KINGS OF THE ROAD

KINGS OF THE ROAD

A PORTRAIT OF RACERS AND RACING

ROBIN MAGOWAN AND
GRAHAM WATSON

SPRINGFIELD BOOKS LIMITED

FOR JOHN WILCOCKSON AND FELIX MAGOWAN

AND IN MEMORY OF KEN EVANS

Text © 1987 Robin Magowan
Photographs © 1987 Graham Watson

Published by Springfield Books Limited,
Norman Road, Denby Dale, Huddersfield
HD8 8TH, West Yorkshire, England

First edition 1987
First paperback edition 1988

British Library Cataloguing in Publication Data
Magowan, Robin
Kings of the Road: portrait of
racers and racing
1. Bicycles. Road racing
I. Title   II. Watson, Graham
796.6'2

ISBN 0-947655-20-4

Parts of this book first appeared, in altered
form, in *Bicycle Action, Cyclist Monthly,
Velo News* and *Winning.*

Cover picture: Bernard Hinault
leads 1986 Tour de France winner
Greg LeMond on the Alpe d'Huez climb
Frontispiece: Greg LeMond after an epic
Paris-Roubaix

Design: Douglas Martin
Typesetting: Armitage Typo/Graphics Ltd
Huddersfield
Printed and bound in Japan by
Dai Nippon Printing Co. Ltd.

CONTENTS

Part One · Introduction

The Kings and Their Sport

BICYCLE ROAD RACING is the national summer sport of most of Europe and South America and for a number of years has been the fastest growing sport in Britain, Ireland and the United States. Greg LeMond's victory in the 1986 Tour de France, Sean Kelly's emergence as the world number one and increasing TV coverage by the major networks all ensure that this trend is going to continue. Nonetheless, this grittiest, most emotionally rending and beautiful of the endurance sports remains barely understood, if at all, by the general public.

In *Kings of the Road* we intend to rectify this situation by showing, from a point of view as close to the rider-gladiator as possible, what bicycle road racing looks and feels like at the top professional level: the roads, the mountains, the constant battle against the mud, heat, rain, snow and wind; the relaxed cheerfulness of the fans – it's one sport where you don't have to pay, and it shows – as well as their harrowed, tearful involvement; the spectacular accidents, riders looking up, bewildered, numbed, or a whole half-pack scythed down on a 120 kmph descent; the moments of finish-line elation and pain; and intimate portraits of the men who make up the professional peloton.

In the course of the succeeding pages, you will come to know what the sport is about, where the riders come from, what motivates them and how they train, as well as the whole chess-like array of moves and counter-moves that preoccupy them. You will learn what is the nature of a race, how races differ and complement one another depending upon terrain, national attitudes, length (single-day classics or several-day stage events), and to a certain extent history – for in a road race the landscape is more than just beauty or obstacle. Each strategic point bears witness to something – a crash, a breakaway, a betrayal – and this past cannot help but influence what is currently taking place.

An Epic Sport

Bicycle racing differs from every other sport I know in being the only one to have been created by writers. One can see why someone is needed to make sense of the whole thing. Imagine a sport that sprawls for days, weeks, maybe almost a month, over a sizable stretch of countryside; where the main action takes place far from where most people live; a race in which the only real witness is the landscape; and you begin to understand how a deliberately created epic sport came into being – one that from the

Francesco Moser leads Roger de Vlaeminck in the 1982 Tour of Flanders

first invited comparison with *The Iliad, The Voyage of the Argonauts,* or the *Song of Roland.* After the announcement of the first race by its sponsoring newspaper, *L'Équipe,* a questing band of men gradually assembled – the knights and squires of the new machine age from whom incredible feats of skill, courage and endurance would be demanded. On the designated day they set out to ride as fast as they could from one city to the next.

And as if the elemental confrontation were not enough, each stage required a separate feat: the cycling on a road spattered with nails; the climbing of a mountain more associated with bears than shepherds; the racing over the cobbled 'hell of the north', with its slippery, mud-drenched setts dating back to the Napoleonic era. It is easy to see why anyone completing such a course, on a bicycle they themselves had to repair, would be called a giant and given a true hero's welcome.

A COMMERCIAL VENTURE

Since its inception in 1869 cycle racing has always been a commercial vehicle, existing to sell newspapers, bicycles and bicycle components. For the newspaper organizing a long-distance race, what was being sold was a feat: a stage race that smacked of the legendary, of epic journeys and far-off battles, could make for compulsive reading. For the fans themselves, besides the beauty of the sport and the emotions they were witnessing, there was the added hope that what they were seeing would turn out to be history: 'We were there that day when...'

However, we can't know whether what we have stood on the road and seen is history – or just another race – until we pick up our paper next morning and discover its significance. And not only was the organizing newspaper able to judge the feats authoritatively, but it could get us hooked by taking us behind the scenes into a world to which it alone held the key. That the sport's protagonists were ordinary-sized people, rather than the monsters of basketball or American football, made their triumphs something we too could vicariously share.

The manufacturer, for his part, wanted as infernal a course as possible, one that would test the mettle of the rider and his chosen mount. It was this combination of sponsoring newspaper and bicycle manufacturer that created a heroic sport, one that in the right circumstances can move us to feelings of awe and compassion.

Unfortunately professional bicycle racing is an expensive sport. For this reason some form of trade sponsorship has always been required to pay the salaries of the riders and their various supporting personnel – managers, mechanics, masseurs and doctors – as well as provide the equipment. Besides the bicycles themselves these include the cost of two team cars and an equipment van or bus. Add entry fees, transportation costs, accommodations, and one gets a figure of close to three million dollars for a team like Panasonic or La Vie Claire.

These trade teams have always been advertising vehicles, run out of a company's publicity budget. This subjects them to the fortunes of business, and a team will be dropped once its cost outweighs the rise in sales that it may bring. Until the mid-1950s teams were sponsored wholly by cycle or cycle accessory manufacturers. But then a massive change-over in personal transport brought a retrenchment that made it look as if the bicycle, and not the oil-dependent car, was doomed to extinction. In desperation riders turned to sources outside the trade to pay for the vast amount of back-up that had become increasingly required. These outside sponsors were not so much interested in the tactical complexities of racing as in the heroes that the sport had created. In countries with a national television that prohibited advertising backing a cycling team could be a good way of getting around the restrictions and ensuring a wide popular recognition for your product.

Despite the difficulties and expense of filming, cycling has become in recent years increasingly involved with television. There are some like film producer Steve Tesch (*Breaking Away* and *American Flyers*) who would go so far as to claim that bike racing is the ideal TV sport because cyclists go fast enough *en masse* to create an atmosphere of excitement and danger, and yet slow enough for the viewer to see the expressions on their anguished faces. While you can see pain on a marathon runner's face, there is little action or speed; and at the other end of the scale, ski and motor racing are so fast that the participants lose their human dimension and are seen as objects rather than real people. Cycling falls in between. For many viewers the Alexi Grewal–Steve Bauer duel in the men's road race of the Los Angeles Olympics constituted the most exciting event in the whole Olympics. There was action and speed all through the event, you could see the anguish on Grewal's face give way to consternation as he was passed by Bauer on the last hill, then his joy at beating the unbeatable Bauer in the sprint for the gold medal. It was very good TV.

BEAUTY AND BRAVERY

To an outsider the first impression a race gives is one of speed and harmony: the silver rush of spokes of an advancing pack; the banked angles of the cornering rider; the tension of the wrists; the steel-eyed, wheel-thin concentration. But unlike most such sports speed here does not lead inevitably to violence. It may happen, but it is not what we are gathered at this turn of the road for, as it palpably is at a motor race. This is why when the crashes occur we don't feel exultant, but sick as if something in ourselves has been bloodied. In cycle racing the rider is not distanced from us by a metallic capsule in which robots could be performing for all we know, but is visually close and extremely vulnerable. In a sculpture of a rider, for instance, we recognize his profession by his helmet, where it indicates his bravery rather than a god-like invulnerability.

These feelings might seem exaggerated were not cycling so directly concerned with beauty. To be sure, so are many other sports, and beauty is itself a term for a rather complex succession of shocks. But cycle racing exists commercially with a primary aim of making us feel the perfection of jersey, of bicycle, to which the rider lends himself, with a masculine beauty far more encompassing than the usual centaur image. From the waist down there is probably no handsomer sportsman.

The usual time to see riders is before the start of a race. As they mill about, signing the start sheet, squeezing lemons and other fruit into the sweet tea of their water bottles, talking to journalists and signing autographs, it is possible with the aid of a

Beautiful legs run into a sea of stones in Paris-Roubaix

programme to study them and fit numbers to a reputed name, a face, seeing what these modern centaurs share in the way of a build, a costume. The riders will have risen perhaps four hours earlier, had a breakfast after their national fashion, followed by a substantial meal. A cursory massage of a few slaps to the legs – (legs are oiled if it is below 60°) – and the riders are off, some on their bikes, others in their team cars, to the site of the start.

While height varies from the 5 ft 2 ins of Vicente Belda to the 6 ft 5 ins of Ralf Hofeditz, most of these 'giants' are a European average, 5 ft 8 ins or so. Legs are shaved and glistening from the massage and, before hard use has set in, there is nothing more athletically beautiful, with the calf muscles not bulging as in soccer players, but descending vertically into arrow-like points. As the rider ages the muscles become more developed and knotted and varicose veins will start appearing, blue signs of what is being endured, stretched. A beautiful sport can quickly become a very cruel one. Upper bodies are less special, superficially resembling the torsos of dancers, with everything that must be carried honed away in defiance of gravity. Riders climb and sprint with their arms almost as much as with their legs, but the gain in power that comes from muscle development never compensates for the added weight that has to be carried. In building themselves up riders try for muscle tone. It can be a very fine line.

Despite a general ranginess, and a desired legs to upper body ratio that favours the longer-legged and short-torsoed, riders are strikingly defined, and limited, by their build. The deep chest cavity of men like Britain's Barry Hoban or Belgium's Rik Van Looy makes for a sprinter. Climbers are either small like Belda or built on the giraffe-like lines of Pascal Simon (though tall riders are limited in that they don't corner well on the descents). In the same way time trialists are generally stockier, more powerfully built. Cyclists may all look as as if they have sprung from a common mould, but once you have compared them up close it is much easier to understand the nature of their achievements. And for the cyclist himself such a niche is important; it gives him a speciality from which he can expand. Making the grade as a general all-rounder is much more problematic. In this connection it is worth pointing out the number of those who at the age of eighteen were already fully developed—Hinault, LeMond, Merckx, Saronni. In a sport where no-one normally signs a pro contract until twenty-one (in Belgium not until twenty-two until recently), such precocity stands out.

Seen against the luminous, coral fish colours of the polyester-coated jerseys, the Lycra cuissards or shorts are uniformly black and lined with a chamois leather crotch. Hands are protected from falls and the friction of the taped handlebars by a sort of golfer's half-glove with perforated holes. Odd in a profession where weight counts for so much are the large wrist watches; less something useful, one suspects, than a reminder of where the battlefield lies. Shoes are stiff and heel-less with cleated soles that ensure that all the rider's power is transmitted directly to the pedals. Off the bike, they make for an awkward, penguin-like gait. But then riders may need to be reminded that their legs are for other things than walking about. This is why, whenever you see them, they are propped up somewhere, in bed or the back of a team car. They don't walk. One incident from the 1986 Coors Classic proves the point: Bernard Hinault is resting at a hotel on the rest day; he turns on the bedroom television and sees his La Vie Claire teammate Greg LeMond playing golf *live* before the cameras. 'How', he asks, 'can a serious cyclist be playing golf on a rest day? He's got to get off his legs...'

On the road the rider becomes a streamlined glistening in the wind, beneath the great back-curved sky, the body stretched out long and dome-like with only the raised head intent above the handlebars. In the river of his concentration it is we rather, the bits of jagged human branch lining and narrowing a climb, who stick out. This crowd, unnerving as it sometimes is, the fan about to push or rabbit-punch him, the dog or child that may at any moment scoot out, can become a second motor under his skin,

An allée of plane trees guides the Paris-Nice race to the south

Tour of Flanders, 1983

removing the particles of soul-destroying monotony, the need to finish merely to go on to the next stage.

This feeling of being chained to a route can be dispiriting and one understands why many have preferred to retire to that farm, factory, or mine, while they still have a semblance of health. But suffering, experience, is, after all, what we ask of life and it is instructive to meet former riders like Van Looy – the Sean Kelly of the 1960s – for whom every start represented a new adventure. Just as a writer can be judged by his disciples, so can a sport be judged by the personalities it has formed.

On a race it is not always easy to talk to the riders; they need their nine to ten hours of sleep. But in the hotel lobbies, the wayside restaurants, one can meet riders who have become journalists, team managers, small entrepreneurs. It is hard to say what has done it, the travel, the constant risk with its stripping away of inessentials, but their presence rings with a humility and a joy in life, a willingness to talk day and night about their former *métier*, such as one rarely encounters.

A sport like cycling almost defies the imagination. If it is beautiful it is because of the riders and the rural landscape they are pitted against. Any sport that allies beauty to bravery in such a degree cannot help but move us. That we can't do it ourselves doesn't mean that we can't stand on the road and applaud and weep for those who can.

THE SOCIAL BACKGROUND

Cycle racing has always been a professional sport. In the days of Helen of Troy a beautiful face may well have launched a thousand ships, but when your efforts are only contributing to a journal's circulation battle, or the sale of bicycles, you may feel you have a right to demand, on top of prize money and such, a daily wage.

Professional roadmen generally come from the urban working classes or, more commonly, their rural equivalent, the small freeholders and landless peasants. This is the same school of suffering from which boxers have traditionally hailed; an analogy that goes a long way to explain the gladiator mentality common to both professions. In both cases the sport represents a way out of a life of hard work and grinding poverty. Talk to any professional cyclist and he will tell you exactly how the sport has enabled him to lift himself socially and enjoy opportunities that would never have occurred had he stayed at home.

Most cyclists start riding at sixteen or seventeen. They turn professional between twenty-two and twenty-three and are generally retired by the age of thirty (a climber, because of his smaller physique, can sometimes go on until his mid-thirties). The average professional career, however, usually lasts no more than three and a half years. This is partly because the competition is so intense – there are a thousand racing amateurs for every professional – and partly because the sport at this level is so hard on one's health.

HEALTHY – OR NOT?

People tend to think of cycling as one of the best ways of staying truly healthy. In supporting the rider the bicycle enables him to put all his energy into moving it forward.

Riders like Sean Kelly still take a hand in the fields during the winter months

Every single muscle, except the sexual, is used, while the pumping motion of the legs allows the blood to be constantly recirculated through one's system. This is why pro cyclists' pulses are so low, averaging 40 beats a minute. But six to seven hours a day, or 20,000 miles a year, is a bit long to be in the saddle and at the professional level cycle racing is definitely not a healthy activity. One has only to look at the riders' faces after a long stage race to see how drawn they are, with their glazed eyes and skin stretched tight against the contours of their skull. Since every muscle is used, every one hurts. Feet swell up in the heat. Hands ache from all the pounding, the constant need to grip. The saddle, narrow beak that it is, quickly becomes one more instrument of torture. Arms and legs may be supported, allowing you to do this daily marathon, but there is nothing to support the lower back. One thinks of climbing as painful, but riders complain almost as much about the descents, the pain across the chest, hands lacerated by the constant gripping on the brakes. Then there are the crashes, inevitable when there are so many riders jammed elbow to elbow within a few yards. And bones, once broken, do not always snap back into the exact same place. In addition to all this there are the alimentary problems in a sport where food is fuel, where you have to be able to feed on the road and retain what you take in.

All this is exacerbated by the gladiator mentality. As a sport road racing thrives on impossibly cruel conditions; the worse the rain, snow, hail and blistering heat, the greater the glory to be won. If you start a race, you are expected to finish it, no matter how gory a mess you may look. In a long stage race like the Tour de France it is not at all rare to see a good half of the pack covered in plasters. However sick, feverish, diarrhetic you are, you have to keep pedalling in the hope that whatever is ailing you will go away. The secret of any rider's survival inevitably boils down to that cliché of any interview, 'I recover well.' In a sport where the riders are pedalling advertisements, decked out from

Cycling can damage your health, too: a pain-killing injection for Colombian Pacho Rodriguez in the Tour of Spain

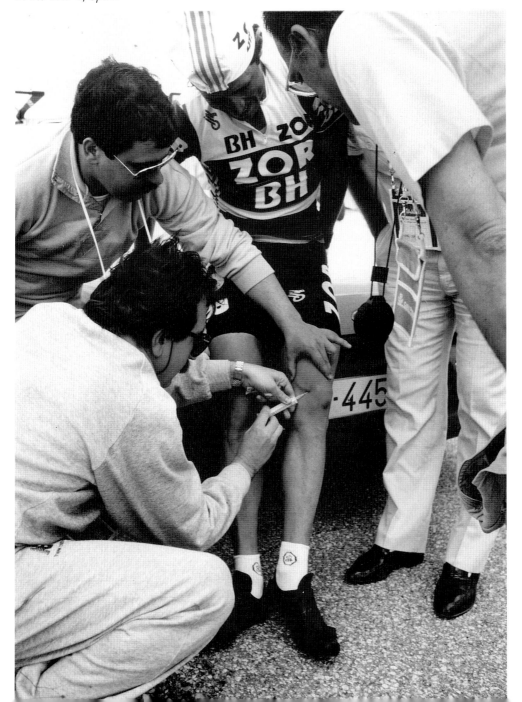

cap to shoes in an unending spiral of names and company logos, you have to be able to display yourself, or be out of a job. And there is very little margin for sickness in the current age of minimal eleven to fourteen man squads. (Most major events feature ten-man teams.)

No matter how careful a rider is about his diet and hygiene, the effects of all the travelling, the constant elemental exposure, are bound to take their toll as the exhaustion builds up in the course of a season. Certain of the more common ailments such as bronchitis or hay-fever cannot be treated without running foul of the drug laws. Run down, and struggling to survive, a rider may find himself turning to the worst possible drugs, the cortisones and steroids, because they can't be so easily detected, taking the cortisone internally as a pain-killer and using steroids as a way of building himself up and countering weight loss. Such abuse eventually takes its toll: one reason why a professional career lasts the few years that it does, and why many pro cyclists die well ahead of the national mean (at an average of fifty-six, according to the World Almanac).

ALL IN THE MIND

Racing at any level requires a considerable commitment. You have to train, and train seriously, and that cuts into whatever else you are trying to accomplish. The 'nothing to lose' social background is helpful in explaining why a kid from the other side of the tracks might want to take a chance and see how far he can go with his talent. But there is also a psychological mentality that a number of riders share and which makes them different from most sportsmen.

With certain exceptions (like Eddy Merckx) cyclists tend to have been rather mediocre sportsmen, with more grit than talent. Some will have come to cycling from other endurance sports, such as cross-country running, speed skating, even swimming (though that gives them a difficult body to shed). For most, though, it is the one sport they have ever been able to do at all well. It becomes thus a revenge on all the others and, because of the hardness and danger, a source of secret pride. Allied to this lack of success at other sports is a psychological quirk one can't help but notice: a great many cyclists are loners, romantic solitaries. And one can see what a great sport cycling is for the loner, all those long hours out by yourself in beautiful countryside, peeping over the stone walls and enjoying the constant changes of scenery. For the cyclist, as for certain joggers, there is an addiction that builds up which has something to do with the increased blood flow to the brain. In any strenuous physical exercise the brain starts to produce endorphins – a relative of morphine – to help give the body an analgesic cushion. This cyclist's 'high' corresponds to the runner's 'third wind'. 'First you pedal until everything hurts – your back, legs, everything,' one friend explained. 'Then it just gets so easy.'

The exercise also allows you to purge all those elements of bad humour and nervous tension. At the end of a couple of hours in the saddle you come in, relaxed and

English amateurs encounter snow conditions in an early February race

at peace. What can be more addictive finally than a sport that allows you to like yourself! At the same time comes a camaraderie with all these others who are experiencing it too for the first time. And it's not surprising that cycling turns around the notion of a club. You can't race without one and the club – the other members, the institution – provide sources of information, help of one sort or another, as well as a first social organism that you can totally accept. It allows you in this sense to come in out of the desert of your adolescence. Here in this context you can like yourself. And it's lovely to see how transformed riders are talking to one another, how open they are, curious about places, roads, each other's quirks, and, like boxers, how unwilling they are to bad-mouth one another. It's a hard profession and riders, like the people watching them along the road, tend to respect everyone who does it.

All those years of isolation have given the rider a certain steel. He is used to being out there, on his own, struggling. This allows him to bear things – the boredom, the danger, the incessant nomadism – that others would find intolerable. The rest depends on how fit and strong he is, and how much he is willing to sacrifice to mastering his profession. We have alternatives, he doesn't. Everything, even the person he marries – where else can he meet her? – will probably have to come from within the sport, generated out of his career.

AMATEUR RACING

Though it is possible to begin racing at fourteen, or even younger, most start at a comparatively advanced sixteen or seventeen. Since they are still growing, distances are not very long, 120 km at most. Their club will usually have a coach, or older riders who can advise them about frame sizes, saddle and shoe-plate position, and all the rest of a highly arcane subject. If they are good, they will quickly get some form of sponsorship, a bike that they may be able to keep, tyres and clothing (otherwise racing can become rather expensive). The coach may also suggest other forms of racing, such as track or cyclo-cross, that will improve their bike-handling so that they will feel more at ease in a cornering bunch and be able to avoid, or ride their way through, a tangle of crashed bikes.

However successful they are at the junior level, the change at eighteen to senior racing is difficult because they are competing against fully grown men at distances often double anything they have ridden. And the style of riding here – all out from the moment the flag drops – is purposely designed to burn them off. To avoid being dropped they may find themselves pushing bigger gears than are good for their still growing bodies.

In amateur racing there is nothing of that slow-slow, quick-quick rhythm that distinguishes professional racing. A 150 km race can be ridden all-out, whereas one 50 to 100 km longer has to be raced in spurts. What usually happens in amateur racing is that the good riders get together and pound along in a big gear as fast as they can. It's only when almost everyone has been dropped that the real manoeuvring starts.

Hinault leads Anderson, LeMond and Herrera on the climb to Pontarlier in the Vosges

At the top of the amateur pyramid, on both the junior and senior level, is a place on the national team and the chance to compete internationally. This is the ultimate form of sponsorship, and coaching, and these places are very much sought after. At a world championships, besides the road racing team, there are four places at stake in the 100 km team time trial and, on the track, in pursuit and four-man team pursuit (which can suit a time triallist). National team selection can be a very good door through which to enter the professional ranks, provided one has not been held back too long.

PROFESSIONAL RACING: FIRST STEPS

For the beginner the most difficult part of professional racing is the distance. It takes a considerable while to build up one's legs to the extra demand. This is the major reason why so very few newcomers achieve anything in their first year or two of racing. Then the style of racing, in spurts, and with the last three-quarters of an hour thundering along at 60 kmph (37 mph), or some 10 kmph faster than the individual world record, is not something an amateur will have ever experienced. Just getting the rhythm of it right, knowing how the attacks may or may not follow one another, and which has a chance of succeeding, takes time.

No matter what name a pro has made for himself as an amateur, the first thing he has to learn is how to be a good team rider or *domestique*. A domestique's main business is to serve his leader, or leaders. He does this by keeping him out of the wind, helping to pace him back to the bunch when he punctures or has to relieve himself, fetching from his team car at the back whatever is needed in the way of equipment, including his own bike if the need arises, capes, extra water bottles, and the rest.

Serving one's leader is more difficult than it sounds, because it involves staying at the front of the bunch and helping shelter him from the wind, as well as doing whatever else he may require. What makes a leader a leader is, partly, that he does have the concentration to ride at the front despite the karate chops of everyone else trying to wedge their way past. Stop pedalling for an instant and you may find that ten riders have gone by you. Stop a bit longer and you may find yourself deep in the shell of the pack. Life back there may be a lot easier than up front because of the air vacuum in which you are riding. But you are also much more liable to be affected and cut off by the sudden speed-up caused by an attack or a crash. Needless to say, all this commuting from leader to team car and back takes its toll.

Besides fetching and carrying and pacing back team-mates who have punctured or been otherwise delayed, a domestique has certain defensive duties. He must help close gaps by taking the wheel of whoever is trying to escape. When a break has already formed he must get in the front line and chase, taking turns with his team-mates in a regular rotation, each taking his 50–100 m stint in the wind. And if his leader or a team-mate has gone away in a solo break he may be asked to slow the chase by interrupting the chasing rotation. But the duties of a domestique are not all onerous. Take the example of a stage race. In the course of chasing down everything that moves, he may

English amateurs riding through the Trough of Bowland in north-west England

Domestique's duties: pushing a team-mate while he answers a call of nature

find himself catching a good breakaway wagon. In this case the domestique will not be allowed to contribute, his only duty consisting of saving himself for the final sprint. Even if he does not win this, as he could (being relatively fresh), he will have gone ahead on general time. A couple of good wagons and he may find himself the best placed rider on his team and thus protected. Getting into a breakaway and being able to contribute is even better. The trick here is to minimize your contribution. A break has to be kept going; but if you do all the work then the others are going to attack you when the right moment comes and seize for themselves everything you have put in. If, however, you have initiated the break, then you have to make sure the others do their part. Otherwise you are carrying along a lot of parasites.

If all riders start off as domestiques, there are many – and some very talented ones among them – who are quite happy to remain in a subservient station so long as their leader keeps winning and the bags of money continue to roll in. They become in this case an extra trump card in a leader's hand, to be unleashed when it suits him, or when he needs to distract everyone's attention. And the domestique may enjoy having the liberty to attack when it suits him, rather than having to be always punctual in the way that a leader must, if he is to have anyone work for him. Perhaps he cannot make himself suffer enough to time-trial well. Or his health is too fragile; there will always be one off day in the mountains. Or he is too much of a lone wolf. Or quite simply he has never known what it is to be truly motivated, to have a leader's shirt on his back and find himself successfully defending it with everything he has got. All sports demand some degree of self-confidence, if one is to succeed in them. But cycling is a sport where it is extremely easy to underestimate yourself. No one knows how much suffering he can take until he has tried it. With a whole highway roaring your name in your ears it may be a lot easier than you ever suspected. Kelly, Criquielion, Fignon and Pollentier riders whose careers changed dramatically with one big victory.

SPRINTING

Once a rider has earned his spurs as a domestique he can think about making a name for himself in one of the three major disciplines: sprinting, time-trialling or climbing.

Sprinting, as a friend describes it, involves a considerable art. 'Head is bent, every muscle you've got is thrown in. Never did man go so fast you think. When you look up, there are fifteen ahead of you. A hard way to make a living.' Nonetheless, it's where much of the prize money lies and explains why sprinters are generally regarded as the aristocrats of the breed. The ability to sprint, like the kick of a track rider, is something a rider is born with and depends on whether he has fast-twitch (sprinter) or slow-twitch (long distance) muscle fibres. How this ability to 'jump' in the last yards of a race into extra gear is cultivated no one can say for sure, but it is something climbers possess as well (only they don't jump so much as surge forward in repeated uphill spurts).

Of all the disciplines, sprinting involves the most conservative mentality, since it is by sitting in and doing nothing to disturb anything that they protect, like a fine wine, their nervous adrenalin. That's why for most of a race they are to be seen deep in the pack where the surrounding bodies form a kind of air bubble that carries them along in such a way that, in terms of energy spent, they are almost freewheeling. Then, with 50 km to go, the jockeying for position begins between those team-mates whose job it is to get you forward and everybody else who is trying to get their sprinter into place; no easy matter in a tightly wedged pack moving at a race-ending 60 kmph. (When a pack is

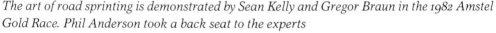

The art of road sprinting is demonstrated by Sean Kelly and Gregor Braun in the 1982 Amstel Gold Race. Phil Anderson took a back seat to the experts

moving at speed it can take twenty minutes to force your way through to the front.)
These prime seats, in the third echelon roughly fifteen to twenty places behind the
windward leader, are hotly contested and the wise sprinter will have already
dispatched forward the two team-mates who will lead him out, with maybe a third
camped on his wheel to prevent some lone wolf from grabbing it and using his
slipstream to flash by in the last metres.

For the sprinter to operate the pack has to be kept intact until the last 500 metres.
This requires considerable team-work in maintaining a pace fast enough to discourage
most breakaways and in jumping on the downwind wheel to close the gap on whoever
is trying to flee. And while one rider is being pulled back, another is jumping away. As
the pack flashes beneath the red 1 km-to-go sign, the sprinter tries to stay just behind the
two who will lead him out: the first launching the sprint between 400 and 600 m, with
the second taking over 300 m from the finish. As the lead-out man begins to fade, 150 m
from the line, the sprinter brings his fast-twitch muscles into play, rocketing off with
such power that some 220 kilos of force are being applied to each thrust of the pedals.
Then, and this is a gift only a few possess, he may re-accelerate once more and, in the
final summation of his art, with an arm movement throw his bike forward on the line.

Just as track has its sprint specialists and quarter-milers, so does cycling have its
short-range *rouleurs* like Jan Raas or Guido Bontempi, invariably big men, who make up
in stamina what they lack in finishing 'kick'. However, a finishing kick doesn't mean
that much when you are going at 60–70 kmph. They are much more useful in criterium
races and small breakaway finishes where the speeds are not all that high to begin with.
What a great sprinter like Bontempi, or 1984 Tour de France Green Jersey Frank Hoste,
has going for him is an uncanny ability to turn a gear 5 kmph faster than the next man.
This ability is called in the trade 'having a higher top-end'.

No less an authority than Sean Kelly, the best all-round cyclist from 1983 onwards,
has noted that there is no such thing as a 'straight' sprinter. With so much money on the
line a rider has to be prepared to fend for his life as well as do whatever is necessary to
make himself respected. The mayhem in the last 100 metres with riders perhaps
grabbing jerseys, catapulting one another, veering out of line and squeezing one another
into the barricades is such that one can understand why most riders are content to leave
the business of bunch finishing to the acknowledged masters of the art. If you fall
in a sprint, you may die, as the 42-year-old Portuguese Joachim Agostinho did when
upended in a crash caused by a dog while leading the 1984 Tour of the Algarve.

TIME-TRIALLING

Finishing speed is often enough to decide a classic or single-day race. But in a stage race
of several days determined on overall time, rather than a points system, one may need
an individual race against the clock to decide the overall winner. The ability to ride a
time trial or 'test of truth' requires a very different talent from that of the sprinter. While
distances vary from the 4–8 km of a prologue to the 40–80 km of a Tour de France time
trial, the essential requirements are the same: you have to be willing to pound out a big
gear. And the bigger the gear, the more asphalt is being chewed up with each turn of the

Post-Moser time-triallist: Belgium's Eric Vanderaerden in a Tour de France prologue

pedals. This ability to turn a big gear, all alone, without any shelter from the wind, over a considerable distance, requires strength and, because of the suffering involved, great courage. The burden is considerable and the ability to bear it is what separates a team leader like Bernard Hinault from a Jean-René Bernaudeau or a Marc Madiot, a Greg LeMond from a Davis Phinney; riders of comparable talent, but who lack the true time triallist's ability to dip into himself, to suffer. Time-trialing is, like long distance running, an anaerobic activity. This is a matter of courage, of how much is at stake for you in the event itself. Do you really want to go every pedal turn of the way as fast as you can; or is it sufficient just being out there, a contender until this moment?

Then there is the matter, as in every other aspect of this sport, of calculation. How over a long distance do you pace yourself? Do you ride all out from the gun, depending on your pride and the noise of all those around you, yelling out their time-checks, 'You are better than . . . you are ahead of,' to keep you motivated? Or after a fast start, do you keep something in reserve, riding yourself in and only approaching your ultimate limits at a predetermined point, say, a third of the way from the finish? Either way, the time triallist's ideal is to finish with nothing left, so spent that he has to be lifted bodily from his bike. And it may be that the energy drink in his bidon contains substances that help keep him going a little bit longer, unable to register the indications that are telling him that he has strayed into that 'red zone' where one's body starts producing the lactic acid that makes it feel as if one has run into a wall. This happens when one's pulse approaches 180 beats a minute and, to monitor it, many cyclists have a pulse meter on their wrist.

The art of time-trialling is basically a question of setting a pace and holding it. That's why you often see riders standing on their pedals on a hill, because they want to keep their momentum and stay in a single gear. This is no easy matter when the organizer has set the course on a rough, tyre-eating road full of curves, dips, and rises that are constantly challenging you to change gear and thus rhythm. Then there is the matter of riding itself. While keeping to a single, ideally egg-like position (rather like the crouch of a downhill skier), you want to pedal efficiently, applying pressure through the whole of each revolution. And you want to do everything you can to minimize wind-resistance. It is here that a demanding course can favour the smaller rider. No matter how aerodynamically a big rider is tucked, head down almost at his knees, back curved in a great arc, he is going to stick out more in the wind than a small, compactly built rider like Hinault. He will also expend more energy in the hills even though he can use his upper body strength to climb with. Then there is the art of handling curves; why you see racers riding a course before a race, memorizing the sequence of turns the way a skier memorizes the gates in a slalom race. Shave them close enough, LeMond insists, and you can save yourself half a kilometre in a 60 km event. But the last thing a time triallist wants is to hit the brakes and LeMond himself has been known to crash, as he did in the final 1986 Tour de France time trial, which could well have cost him the race.

Until recently a rider's time trial mount was the same as his climbing bike, except that the tyres were wafer-thin. (A number of the better-paid riders keep stacks of tyres

Climbing in the Tour de France: spectators pack the summit at the legendary Tourmalet pass

in their cellars, aging them like bottles of wine.) Following Francesco Moser's 1984 World Hour Record, and on the heels of East German experimentation with a more streamlined type of frame, there has come a technological revolution that, as far as time-trialling is concerned, has virtually done away with the century-old diamond-frame machine with the same size front and rear wheels. One can debate the pros and cons involved in the UCI's (Union Cycliste Internationale) approval of new disc wheels; of 'progress' as against the prohibitive expense that limits the equipment to a moneyed few. But when it is a question of being able to pedal a second and a half faster per kilometre, there are few time triallists who would not want a pair of disc wheels, rigid and ungainly as they are.

CLIMBING

In English, climbing sounds as natural as walking. You turn out your toes, stick out your arms, and some ancestral monkey presumably takes over. The French 'grimper' (to climb) gives more of what it must feel like on a machine never intended for such usage, as if your teeth were being slowly ground into a spine hunched at such an angle that any sucking in of air becomes exceedingly problematical.

If man was never intended to climb – on a bike – there are nonetheless some whose lightness of body allows them to defy gravity better than others. These are the climbers and in cycling they come in a variety of shapes and sizes, from hopping fleas to scrambling goats to long-legged giraffes to effortlessly soaring winged angels. While climbing is an art that can be learned, demanding suppleness, a technique of spinning your legs rather than churning a gear, the ability itself to a very large extent depends on your lung capacity or VO_2 max, with which you are born. Also a true climber has a distinctly jerky gait of his own that makes it impossible for someone who climbs evenly to take his wheel. And it is amazing to watch a Robert Alban or Robert Millar sprint forth from a lead platoon as though shot from a large bore cannon.

The climbers have their own fraternity with its subtle gradations; those, for instance, who climb on the odd rather than the even chain ring. In the mountains it is hard to eat normally because the hands are never free and because it is harder in the heat to take in food and digest it except in liquid high calorie form. Meanwhile, because one is sweating one's demands for liquid are inordinately high. The possibility of the 'bonk' and with it one's whole season melting away is well understood by the climbers, who are always ready to share a bidon, and by the general populace who are there partly so they can help, offer a bit of water or, better, because there is no chance of its being spiked, a can of coke.

A race in the flat is like a dance with endless permutations on a basic slow, slow, quick-quick rhythm. And the pack, this 200-headed hydra insatiably gobbling up every

Stephen Roche leaving Laurent Fignon behind on the climb of Haute Levée in Liège-Bastogne-Liège

following pages: The 1986 Tour de France snaking its way up the 2850 m Col du Galibier

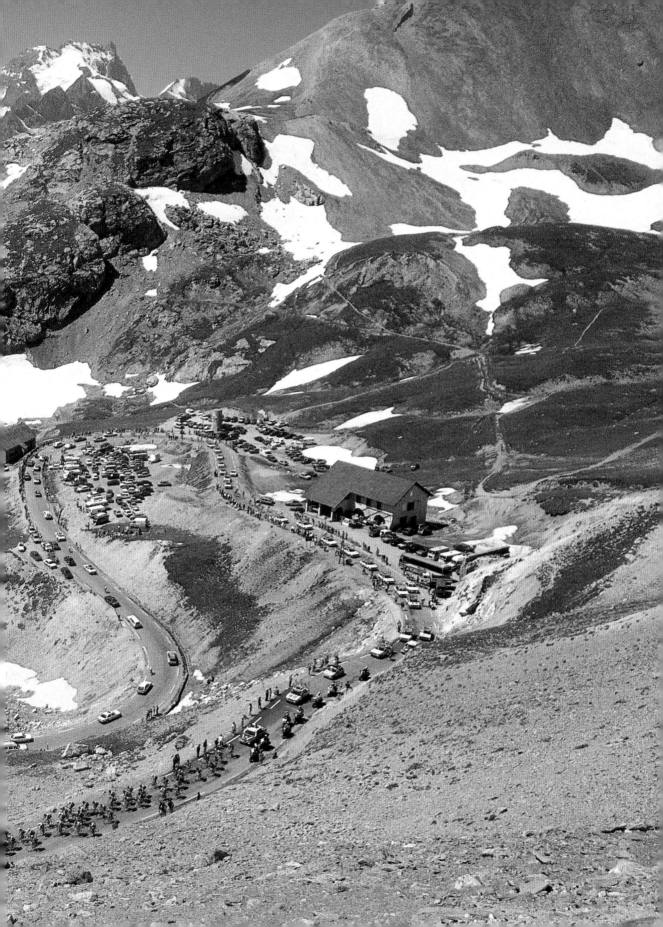

attempt at an escape, remains very much the governing monstrosity. In the mountains, at the first touch of a true gradient, the pack instantly disintegrates, as if dynamited by a master blaster. Elements of it may reform on the down-slope, or a succeeding flat, but it will disintegrafe again on the first slopes, dispersing into smaller and smaller knots the higher the climb goes.

One of the reasons the pack is dynamited is that at climbing speeds there is little draught and every rider is to a large degree riding his *own* time trial against the mountain. There is also quite a bit of pressure being applied by those who have most at stake, the climbers. During most of the racing in the flat they will have bided their time, keeping their energy reserves intact in the air-sealed bubble of the pack, and letting what skirmishes there are rage without them. But at the first sight of a true slope there is a general rush to get forward on the part both of the climbers and those trying to burn them off before they can bring their natural advantages into play. Meanwhile those stranded, who have 'gone out the back', must try to organize themselves into a train in the hope of beating the rule in a stage race that requires that everyone must finish within a certain percentage of the winner's time or be expelled from the race.

Unnatural as it may be to assault a mountain on a bike, it is here that the sport truly comes into its own. On the highest of the Tour de France's mountains, the Galibier, with the whole world seemingly spread beneath you, you feel you know exactly where Christ was taken when he was tempted by the devil. All around are these white-wigged eminences, defying, separating, and as always judging. Then again everything for once is distinctly visible. All a spectator has to do is pick a flower-lit bend near the summit, take out his picnic basket, and wait. It may even help to walk about a bit, experience what 100° degrees of sun are doing to this stove-top on which you stand. Then for an hour or so, at a third of their normal speed, singly, in pairs, in small groups, the riders will come by, the last struggling just as much not to be eliminated as the first are struggling with the moment of their life, if not a whole next year's pay-cheque. Once they have passed, you can clamber back into your car, if you are a journalist, and start following them, catching the cadaverous, haunted looks, the winks, 'I'm not as bad as I look', as now and then you overtake them.

Where in the countryside the spectators normally appear in small isolated clusters, here in the mountains they are wedged together like a seabird colony on a cliff. The police estimated that there were 250,000 alone in 1986 on L'Alpe d'Huez, or ten for every metre of roadway from the end of the valley to the ski station finish. The higher you go, the narrower is the cyclable aisleway, one amateur photographer after another staying down in the very path of the wheels until the last possible second before leaping away. And they have been known to miscalculate, not to have allowed for that press car slightly larger than all the others, and which passes to a scream of mangled feet.

By the last uphill finish the emotions verge on absolute hysteria. At every turn of the pedal seconds are ticking away, you have to give every last bit or face the consequences. And most of those watching, clutching their copies of *Winning* or *Wielerevue*, dressed in their cycling garb, will understand exactly what the

Sean Kelly faces up to the climb of the Madonna del Ghisallo during the 1985 Tour of Lombardy

consequences are for each rider both in the immediate race and for his career at large.

The excitement has much to do with where the mountains come in a race. For a week, possibly longer, the Tour de France riders will have been approaching this crucial pass; now they are here. Every one of them, no matter who he is, is being clapped, cheered, wept for. People in bathing suits, with great bellies and weird hats, are running about, shouting, pouring water. Riders who have run out of fuel are helplessly weaving from one side of the road to the other. One or two may have even stopped, put their foot down. Others have not only gone through the 'wall', but in a number of cases look as if they have passed onto the other side. Quick, if you don't catch them now, they will fall off the cliff! And no matter how illegal, or how much the pushed rider is being fined in seconds, some of the spectators do catch them, holding them upright as their bike starts to spin out of control, giving them a running push so that, clipped into their toestraps as they are, they can start pedalling again. Some riders are even pushed up entire mountains, from one set of hands to the next.

We know why men go off to war. It is harder to explain why a few might want to attempt a profession in which the suffering is so internalized. Are they masochists? If not, why the hell are they doing it? Here in the mountains the question becomes suddenly luminous. One has only to look around: at the awesome surroundings; at the millions gathered so far from where they live; and at these little figures approaching up the vertiginous bends of a pass. There is something called glory and here on these heights these riders are in the process of attaining it. As a reaching down into oneself there is probably nothing more masculine. To see them, whoever they are, being challenged, changed before your eyes is a rending experience. An epic sport has come into its own.

THE PEUGEOT FOREIGN LEGION

What drew me initially to the Tour de France in 1978 was an event which I saw as an ongoing national festival, a test of life. In the course of following it I discovered something quite different – a unique epic sport. And this sport with its insistence on will, with its disparity between the riders' social backgrounds and the heroic nature of the feats they are required to perform, with its signal beauty and courage and openness to adventure, very much moved me. At the same time I could not help but be aware that the epic event I was seeing was itself dwarfed by something very much larger and, to my way of thinking, rather more attractive – a season. It was this, stretching from early February to mid-October, that formed the basis of the riders' professional existence. If I wanted to know them and their sport it was this season in all its far-flung variety that I would somehow have to see.

This was, I came to understand, no easy matter. Races are much reported; they are little seen, a time trial or a mountain interlude aside. A photographer, strapped onto the back of a motorcycle, may be lucky enough to catch an incident or two in the process of skirting a pack – and his comments are invaluable. A journalist riding ahead in the left lane (the right is reserved for the team cars, who of course have precedence) may hear details of the attacks, punctures and so forth on the race radio. But he sees virtually nothing except in the rare case of a breakaway with more than a minute's advantage. At such times one may well believe that the one guaranteed way of not seeing a race is to attempt to follow it in a press car.

One way out is to have a point of access within the peloton; or several such, since the riders themselves can only see what is going on in their immediate vicinity. Acquiring this is difficult because the riders' time is acutely circumscribed. They are either in the saddle, or in a car, or in bed. To get them to talk in what time they may have you have to gain their confidence, no easy matter in a closed society. No matter what, certain subjects such as drugs will remain taboo. Without some knowledge of how much they are making in salary, team bonuses, appearance fees and the like, it is hard to fathom the trade-offs that operate within a race and which so often determine why a breakaway succeeds. Then, as in all professions, there is a coded language which assumes a certain complicity. If your mouth has not been sealed in advance, you are apt not to get very far. Still, in a sport as publicity-conscious as cycling a reporter has a definite leverage. For one thing, riders are paid largely in terms of the number of inches of newspaper copy they generate in a season. It is in their interest to be better understood.

As an American myself I was tempted to turn to the two American professionals making a living on the Continent, Jonathan Boyer and Greg LeMond. But highly sympathetic as they are, I feared that trying to see the sport as either of these riders sees it – and with them one does have to choose – would not give me quite what I needed. Cycling at its best is a team sport and it is that intricacy of competing interests, the various combinations, legal and illegal, that I wanted to record. While there were a number of teams one might have chosen I found myself drawn by the range of personalities offered by Peugeot; especially their so-called Foreign Legion, made up of Irishman Stephen Roche, Australians Philip Anderson and Allan Peiper, Scot Robert Millar, and Englishman Sean Yates. If none were as yet exactly household names, they presented an impressive array of talent, and one capable of bringing a new spirit into professional cycling. All five of these riders had come up the same way, racing as amateurs for the Peugeot-supported ACBB in the Paris suburb of Boulogne-Billancourt and from there progressing to Peugeot as professionals.

It is clear that a kid arriving in Paris from Melbourne, or for that matter Dublin or Glasgow, with no money and no ability to speak French, has a different motivation from the amateur who races out of his family home. He has more at risk – he is cutting himself off from his culture, his chances of education – and as a result a much greater belief in himself. Not everyone can make the transition; but one can see that those who do are already suited for the nomadic life of a professional cyclist. And because they have to earn their place in a squad, event by event, they are more apt to regard cycle racing as a sport than a trade. This also influences their attitude towards money. Where the continental's main concern is to create a regional name for himself, one that will allow him to open a local restaurant or bike shop, or work in public relations, the expatriate has to make his money on the spot, in a signally brief career. If this properly mercenary attitude causes hackles to rise here or there, or evokes a nationalist backlash, that's all part of the price he's prepared to pay.

In a sport where local knowledge and crowd support can be determining it may seem surprising that these English-speaking riders should have succeeded to the extent that they have, Graham Jones, Robert Millar and Stephen Roche winning the overall French amateur points championship in consecutive years from 1978-80. Sean Yates and Allan Peiper might well have followed suit if the rules had not been changed to bar foreigners from the points championship. This apparent domination has to be qualified, as Yates has pointed out, by the fact that the ACBB imports were full-time cyclists. At

Allan Peiper of Australia: one of Peugeot's 'Foreign Legion'

the comparatively short distances of amateur racing the fitter you are, the more likely you are to succeed.

It was only natural that Peugeot should have exercised its prerogative to snap up the best riders from its chief sponsored club: Jones, Millar, Roche, Anderson, Peiper and Yates. There are some, like Peugeot publicity head Pierre Boudot-Lamotte, who would like to claim that this internationalism represented a conscious marketing choice; betting on a young rider in the hope that he might be of help in penetrating a foreign market. My own hunch is that Peugeot was just doing what circumstances demanded. You don't go to the expense of supporting a club only to see your best products skimmed off by someone else not when they include that year's national champion! And in those pre-recessionary times having to employ two Frenchmen for every one foreigner cannot have been too much of a burden. One would think that if Peugeot had been conscious of what they were doing they would have made some effort to exploit the image of an Anderson, a Roche, in his home country. And they would have treated them, even in their first year, as something other than pariahs.

Racing for Peugeot was not exactly easy. In addition to the chauvinism, a French word if there ever was one, there was the internecine rivalry caused by too many would-be leaders. For most of 1982 the Peugeot riders spent more of their energy riding one another down than doing what they had to do to win a race. When Roland Berland succeeded Maurice De Muer as manager at the end of 1982 one of the first things he did was to get rid of Jean-René Bernaudeau, Michel Laurent and Graham Jones. Peugeot may still have been lacking true team riders, Bernard Bourreau ('petit frère', as he was aptly known) aside. But to all appearances Roche and Anderson were now free to start concentrating on the opposition.

Getting Peugeot cooperation turned out to be easier than I had expected. The outgoing liaison man between the team and the company, René Beillon, liked my project and invited me to the team's February training camp in Seillans; the one time of the year, he said, when the riders are all together. Before going south I managed to visit Yates, Millar and Roche in their family homes in order to get some idea as to the various pressures, family, environment and other, that go to compose that extraordinary thing, a cyclist's will power, as well as to learn what each had personally at stake in the coming campaign.

Judged by the number of bicycle makers forced into bankruptcy, and the continuing shrinkage of teams and personnel, the 1983 season I witnessed through their eyes hardly seems a banner year. On the racing level, however, I had the impression that I was seeing the birth of a new style of riding, something very different from the blocked races and mass complacency that had prevailed for much of the past twenty years. To appreciate 1983's attacking style it helps to recall 1982, the year of the freak result. On the one hand, there was the lethargy that could permit long escapes of the type that saw Marc Gomez win Milan-San Remo, René Martens the Tour of Flanders. On the other, there was Bernard Hinault imposing his own brand of torpor on the Giro and the Tour de France. That Jonathan Boyer, who had yet to win a professional race, could almost have made away with the world title at Goodwood seems almost typical. It was that kind of a year.

Riders are very much the products of their time. If the prevailing milieu condones mediocrity and defensive riding, who is to blame them for settling for what's easy? Also the habits of twenty-five years, of the blocked race strategy favoured by Anquetil and Merckx, are not easily thrust aside. With the benefit of hindsight one can ask why no-one besides Phil Anderson attacked a distinctly vulnerable Hinault in the 1982 Tour de France; or, more to the point, why was the Australian supported in his efforts to hang on to his Yellow Jersey by only one team-mate, Bernard Bourreau? To say it was a question of combines, of French riders and teams pulling together in defence of what they might see as the national interest, is tempting, but a little easy. It is fairer to say that a good rider like Hinault creates the psychological climate that will allow him to win. If others follow him down the badger hole, so much the better. We know now why Hinault rode such miserly races, parcelling out his rare efforts, calculating each spin of the wheel – because of his suspect knees. But one can also see how such economical riding might appeal to his minions; to the extent where the riders regarded Italian racing, where everything proceeds at parade pace until the last half hour, as the acme of their profession. To a man, almost, it seemed that their purpose in life was not racing, but making money, being what might be called professional. To go all out and attack Hinault would have called their whole *raison d'être* into question and jeopardized what little they had.

But even in cycling voids don't go on forever. Eventually the money runs out and the riders realize that if they are to go on being employed they have got to train properly, treat their profession with the dedication necessary to win races. At the same time the public may get bored with so-called classics that are still serving up the same fare as fifty or eighty years ago when bikes and road surfaces were considerably different.

There is a well-known saying in continental cycling that 'it's the riders who make a race, not the route'. Yes, but they need courses that can encourage their attacks, ones different from the 1982 world championships circuit at Goodwood, or what now passes for Milan-San Remo. Instead in 1982 we were seeing one stage race after another being decided on its prologue times. To defend a few seconds' margin may require good team work. But it is not likely to satisfy a public brought up on the notion of cycling as the hardest, the most truly heroic of the endurance sports.

Sponsors like to talk about bringing racing to the people. All very well, but people tend to live in the flat rather than by the lonely cobbled roads and mountain tops that a race needs if there is to be any attacking. Why not instead encourage the people to use their increasing mobility to come to the mountains? If the race is lively enough the fans will come. There are usually more people watching the Tour de France time trial on the Puy de Dôme in the middle of July – at several pounds a head – than are left in the whole of Paris. Cycling is not the sport it is sheerly out of sadism, but because length and variety of natural difficulties are what a race needs if it is to serve as a true test.

PART TWO · THE KINGS

Following his retirement in 1978, Eddy Merckx changed his racing gear for a business suit

EDDY MERCKX

ONCE A MILLENNIUM a prince comes along who decides that a Macedonia, a Mongolia, is not big enough for him. He wants the whole works. Gathering together his little horde he sets out, conquering and laying waste as he goes along. Great for him and the history writers; not so great for his subjects.

It was this image of the rider-despot that Eddy Merckx represented. His *nom de guerre*, the 'cannibal', may define the way he ate up, made mince-meat of his adversaries. It does not define the extent of his appetite. Most riders limit themselves to certain objectives. They train so that they will 'peak' at that one crucial moment, or span of weeks, the world championships, the spring classics, the Tour de France. Unlike them Merckx wanted it all, from February to October. And once he was there on the starting line he was determined to win. The process, given the odds of a race, the numbers against him, the things likely to go wrong, was for all of us watching extraordinarily exhilarating–how would he do it this time? Between 1966 and 1977 everything fell to him, five Tours of Italy and five Tours de France, every classic except Paris-Tours, the world hour record. Riders before him would win the Super Prestige Pernod award with a total of between 200 and 250 points. Merckx in his heyday would win it with anything between 400 and 550. (Note that the scoring system was changed in 1985.)

For his adversaries such omnipresence could be depressing, riding day after day looking for what crumbs the great man was prepared to throw away. And cycling is not a sport where second place counts. Riding in Merckx's shadow something went out of them, and out of the sport for a while as well; what might be called the notion that on a given day, with all the right elements united, you might enjoy a state of grace in which everything was possible, you all alone on this black, cheering road, the rest of the pack strung out invisible behind you.

With Merckx such days didn't exist, because he did not allow them to. Once one gets it into his head to revolt, others are apt to do the same. If you are going to dominate, you have to do it no matter how unpleasant it is. In the old days it was common practice in a race like the Tour de France to allow a local rider to break away when approaching his home town so that he could ride in alone, put his foot down, embrace in some privacy his wife and child. Merckx saw to it that he was always accompanied and usually by no less a personage than himself.

Merckx was an exception to the rule that cyclists must hail from among the socially disadvantaged. His parents were small shopkeepers in the Brussels suburb of Woluwe-Saint Pierre and Eddy was himself well-educated. (His autobiography, *Coureur Cycliste*, reads like the memoirs of De Gaulle.) Good at sports in a way few cyclists are, he might as easily have made a career in soccer or his favourite, basketball. But at the right age, fourteen, he discovered cycle racing and, with the help of an excellent coach, Félicien Vervaecke, it became his competitive outlet. By eighteen he was the world amateur champion. After turning professional at 19 he went over to Peugeot, for whom he was to win Milan-San Remo twice and the world professional championships in 1967. But the strains of cohabiting with 1967 Tour de France winner Robert Pingeon and Tom Simpson cost him a couple of crucial classics victories. When Peugeot refused to give him the four team riders he wanted, he formed his own team, Faema. With them he won Paris-Roubaix while still two months shy of twenty-two. It is from that moment that his hegemony dates, with victories in the Tour de Romandie and the Giro d'Italia soon following. When a year later he won in the most crushing manner possible the Tour de France a legend was confirmed.

Slightly over 6 ft tall, Merckx was far from the optimum size for a racer who has to climb mountains. And it took him, as he admits, a couple of years before he came up

Joop Zoetemelk

with a bike that allowed him to feel at ease on the descents (on which he fashioned so many notable victories), one reason he did not ride the Tour de France until 1969. But the agility he had already gained from track-riding cannot be over-emphasized. And riding in a fixed gear on the track taught him to spin rather than to pull a gear in the modern fashion (with all the strains that puts on the knees). In the whole of his career he was never in anything lower than a 15.

First-rate coaching in a highly compact environment blessed with a lot of know-how explains a lot. But the secret of this Belgian's great success lies for me in his lucid single-mindedness allied to a ferocious will to win. From the age of sixteen on he knew what he wanted, and he pursued it. No technical detail was too small for him and the fact that he 'retired' into bike manufacturing, determined to give Campagnolo a run for their money, shows something of the fanaticism he brought to choices of seat, saddle position, fork angles and so forth. To me, even more suggestive was his saying, shortly after his retirement in 1978, that even in the moment of receiving a trophy on the podium, he was already envisioning the roads of his next race. Such a keen concentration and real love of the sport has never been seen since. And it's no wonder that his team-mates got caught up in the crusade. Joseph Bruyère, his right-hand man during most of this period, did not want to win the 1978 Tour de France for himself; he wanted to win it for Merckx. When you saw them together, in an elevator, hands around each other's shoulders, that was obvious. That Bruyère came within a whisker of doing it, and never really raced again, shows what risks to his health he was prepared to undertake.

Just as some men are compulsive womanizers, so are there others who feel compelled to win. Merckx's wife Claudine's account of Eddy's face buried in a towel still weeping two hours after his defeat in the Nürburgring world championships in 1966 – he had got cramps in the final lap – could not be more revealing (he won it the next year at Heerlen). The least defeat became a personal insult. But it was the conception of who he was and the sport he represented that was to prove in so many cases the determining motivation. Merckx's winning of Paris-Roubaix in 1968 was his way of atoning for two earlier defeats. But he had to do it that year, he told his wife before leaving for Compiègne, because he had the world champion's Rainbow Jersey on his back and any Belgian would have felt the same with Roubaix so near the border. By the end of his career this compulsion had become almost frightening. The Belgian should probably have retired after the 1975 Tour de France in which he finished second with a broken wrist. Despite having lost his climbing ability he lingered on for another three years in the hope of regaining the form that would allow him to achieve a record sixth victory.

Merckx came into cycling at a crucial time for the sport. There had been the so-called Golden Age of Coppi, Bartali, Kubler, Koblet, Van Steenbergen, Schotte, *et al.* After an interregnum of Bobet, DeBruyne, and Merckx's boyhood hero, Stan Ockers (who discovered himself at thirty-three, won the Worlds at thirty-five and died in a track accident the next year) there had come a ten-year period in which the kingdom was

Lucien Van Impe

basically divided between Rik Van Looy – or Rik the Second as the 'emperor' was known in Belgium (Van Steenbergen was Rik the First) – and Jacques Anquetil. While each held firm sway in his particular domain – Van Looy's was the classics, Anquetil's the stage races – both were basically negative riders. For each, winning was a question of keeping anything from happening; until the last hundred metres in Van Looy's case when he would bring his weapon, the sprint, into play; until the very end for Anquetil who preferred to outdo everyone against the clock.

In this climate one can imagine the resurgence of interest Merckx brought to the sport. One would think fans might find his winning race after race boring. Instead they lined the roads, blacker than ever, waiting for the inevitable attack. And his presence in a race was enough to ensure that it would be hard, run at a brisk enough tempo to burn off the would-be wheel-suckers and eliminate the pure sprinters from the final reckoning. In Merckx's legs the sport of giants was reborn.

It was only natural that when Merckx retired he should leave a gaping hole. People won, but there was always a sense of something missing, a lost panache; we were in an era of dwarves, minor specialists, rather than giants. Gradually, though, a new generation began to gain confidence in itself. We may not be yet in the Golden Age of the post-war decade; but we have had of late a growing number of good races, a sign that the positiveness Merckx brought has by no means vanished. It is with this post-Merckx generation and the challenge of a new style of riding from outside the Continent that the following portraits are concerned.

JOOP ZOETEMELK

In a sport where only first place counts this carrot-haired Dutchman is that rare anomaly, a rider who has made a career of finishing second. Dubbed the 'wheel-sucker' by Merckx, he is now more correctly remembered as the only rider of his generation capable of staying with the great Belgian. Describing his rivals, Thevenet, Ocana, and Maertens, in a recent interview Zoetemelk said, 'They all tried to duel with Eddy. He killed them. I was smarter. I refused to force myself. I knew exactly how far my possibilities reached. The others were prepared to go further than that. For me it was sufficient to stay with him. You can't imagine the strength he had in his legs.'

Nonetheless Zoetemelk is being more modest than the record warrants. Now and then in the hills he outclimbed Merckx and there was a time in 1974 when he was beating him regularly. He had won Paris-Nice by a good margin and looked set to repeat in the Tour de France when in the final tune-up, the Midi Libre, he hurtled into a car mistakenly parked by the finish line and cracked open his temple. To many it is a miracle that he ever walked again, let alone raced a bike. Yet nine months later he was riding well enough to win Paris-Nice: the second of his three victories in the event.

The attempt to come back so quickly may well have overtaxed his system. A few months later he came down with meningitis, lost 22 pounds in a single week and almost died. At the same time the doctors discovered that he had been riding with a double

Eddy Merckx: the world's greatest cycling legend in action during his last Tour de France

Joop Zoetemelk

Zoetemelk time-trialling in the prologue to Paris-Nice in 1983

skull fracture. Zoetemelk somehow recovered from all this, and within only a few months, but the disease took its toll on his health. He never regained the stamina he had before, nor anything like the same day-to-day consistency. As he says, 'Even to this day there is still something wrong with my sense of taste.'

Zoetemelk owed his early stamina to the Dutch national sport, speed skating. As a boy he dreamed of competing not in the Tour de France, but in the Eleven Cities skating race. He did well enough at it to win a regional title as a junior. All speed skaters ride a bike during the summer and Joop soon found himself doing well enough to be invited to join the Mexico Olympics. He went on to win the amateur Tour of Yugoslavia and everyone's apprenticeship for the Tour de France, the Tour de l'Avenir. After turning professional with Flandria he won the Dutch road race title in 1971, a victory he was to repeat two years later.

The team Zoetemelk joined when he came to ride in France was Poulidor's Mercier. How much the experience of riding with Anquetil's eternal second stamped the Dutchman is hard to say; but neither is what you would call talkative, and their mutual affinity as friends, their truly professional dedication, may have masked a lack of imagination, of the fire needed to win races. In Poulidor's case it is said that if you knew the humbleness of his Auvergnat background, you could understand why it was enough for him just to be up there, rivalling Anquetil. For Zoetemelk the same may hold.

At the same time, one should add that in the peloton itself there is no more respected rider. His means may be, as Roche has said, limited. He lacks, for one, any sort of 'jump'–whether as a result of his accident or not I don't know–and thus has trouble getting away. But once he has sufficient space in which to operate, as in a hill time trial, there is no better rider. In the 1976 Tour de France he was the outstanding rider and should have won except for the tactical error he made in underestimating Van Impe. When his second chance came in 1980 he was already over the hill. It was his good luck then, as he freely admits, to be supported by a strong Raleigh team. With their help he was able to get through the inevitable bad patch and win the Tour.

Then during the 1983 Tour, at a time when he was still very much in contention, came Zoetemelk's second steroids penalization. Stung by the injustice, and the slight on a scrupulously built-up reputation, he considered retiring to Le Richemont, the 40-room hotel in Meaux along the Marne that he owns and operates with the help of his wife Françoise, the daughter of a Tour de France executive. But he missed cycling and allowed himself to be persuaded back for a farewell 1985 season. Over the winter he trained especially hard. His early season form was such that he won Tirreno-Adriatico, no mean achievement. And he retained enough of it to be still in contention on the last lap of the Montello world championships after nine-tenths of those starting had departed. The rest is history: Zoetemelk went on to become at thirty-nine the oldest ever World Champion. There are many who are convinced he will, for all his talk of retirement, go on racing until his fifties.

Lucien Van Impe

LUCIEN VAN IMPE

There has always been something enigmatic about this 'impish' Belgian coal-miner's son from Mere; a suspicion that for him there are other things in life besides cycling. When during the winter months everyone else is out building up their endurance on the North Sea roads, Van Impe has always been quite content to stay at home and do his pedalling on a home-trainer before his television set. If he had his career to do over again, he said in a recent interview, he would rather have been a soccer player. And one gathers what he means. For a rider with only one true string to his bow, life must get rather boring out there on the roads between mountains. But football scouts don't come storming to the door of a 5 ft 6 ins player whose legs in no way resemble those of a Diego Maradona. And the open roads of cycling, however bunched and hazardous, must have seemed preferable to a perspective taken from inside a mine-shaft.

Most racers have a number of events that suit them. Van Impe, with a singleness of mind that one can't help but envy, has always limited himself to preparing for one event, the Tour de France. Why this should be, other than that for most of his career he was riding for French teams, is hard to say. One would think the Vuelta, Liège-Bastogne-Liège, the Dauphiné, or the Tour of Lombardy would have suited a climber who was the greatest of his age and a more than acceptable time-triallist. But rather than spread himself Van Impe has preferred to concentrate on an event that he has ridden a record fifteen times, nearly always with distinction.

This single-minded approach has not endeared him to his employers. It is a rare autumn that has not found him casting about for a new team. And his employers' hesitations, their need to wait for mid-November when the Tour itinerary is announced, are understandable. Who knows, it might be a mountainless one, as in 1985, and then where would they be? At the same time it is understandable how the constant changes in team, new and questionable equipment to adjust to, poor quality team riders, might have sapped Van Impe's morale. In such circumstances it is indeed remarkable that in 1983, at thirty-seven, he came very close to repeating his 1976 victory.

In the years before he won the Tour there was the feeling, by no means unjustified, that it was the White Jersey with the red polka dots of the mountain points prize that Van Impe identified with rather than the overall winner's Yellow. Certainly before 1976 there were a number of occasions when he could have won the Tour. But it would have meant risking something and perhaps going out of the race as a result. In this connection Van Impe's almost uniquely unblemished drug test record is not without its relevance. 'Perhaps I could have won more if I had taken something,' Van Impe himself has suggested. It is hard to surmise what held him back. Fears for his health? An unwillingness to experiment? At times one could wish that there had been in Van Impe's breast room for a little Napoleon.

There was, however, to be a Napoleon of a sort in Van Impe's life in the person of his 1976 sports director Cyrille Guimard, who went on to coach Hinault, Fignon and LeMond. In *Un Vélo dans la Tête,* Guimard recounts at exasperated length all he had to do to goad Van Impe into making the most of his one opportunity, prodding him into his three-pass flight, keeping him there . . . Reading it one can see why Zoetemelk could not get himself to believe what Van Impe was in the process of perpetrating, it was so out of character. Or why, despite winning the Tour, Van Impe refused to ride for Guimard any more (he didn't like being talked to that way!). As for Guimard, his reputation by that one single stroke was made.

For myself, though, I admire more Van Impe's efforts the following year to prove he was more than a Guimard clone. All around France for umpteen stages we watched as this little David, looking always in the bloom of health, geared himself up for his one great moment of battle with Bernard Thevenet's Goliath. I was standing on my tiptoes on a steep slanting Paris sidewalk the afternoon when Van Impe decided to attack some 50 km from the Alpe d'Huez finish, on the Glandon. Out of character, maybe, but gripping in its contrast of forces, of styles of riding, as we watched the Belgian, having gambled his all on a good descent, gradually succumb to the valley wind and the superior power generated by the cortisone-charged Frenchman. Suicidal, he should have waited until the foot of the Alpe d'Huez, screamed the papers next morning. But for me it was the first true combat I had seen and beginning to understand their views, their different determinations (Thevenet had to undertake the whole chase on his own, with Kuiper sitting in, waiting to sabotage him), it taught me a lot. It was Van Impe's gamble, that risk-taking against the odds, which I came to admire in Pollentier and again, years later, in Roche, Millar and Anderson.

FRANCESCO MOSER

In a sport so heavily influenced by innovative Italian styling in both equipment and costume, it seems fitting that one of the true kings should be Francesco Moser. This handsome generous-hearted Italian's career is proof that in cycling life does occasionally begin well past thirty. Before that, of course, he had done all right for himself. You don't win the Worlds, the Flèche Wallonne, two Tours of Lombardy, the Super-Prestige Pernod, and *three* Paris-Roubaixs, if you don't have more than a smidgen of talent. As for his courage, one had only to have seen him in Paris-Roubaix, taking the cobbles head-on in his unique high-seated style; or to have watched him in one or another Italian race, pounding along with everyone tucked in behind him.

It was this very example of courage that instilled in Graham Watson the urge to photograph cycle racing, day in, day out, sometimes for weeks on end. Coming into the sport at a time when Merckx was on the verge of retirement, it was Moser to a much greater degree than Hinault who caught Watson's eye, a question of his awesome strength and his indomitable will to overcome his main handicap, his sheer physical bulk. Wherever Watson was, whether on a cobbled 'berg' in Flanders, or a muddy track in Paris-Roubaix, or aboard a motor-bike in a 250-strong Milan-San Remo peloton, it was always Moser he saw forcing the pace.

All the same one can imagine Italian racing becoming dispiriting after a certain number of years of towing all those leeches about, even if you were, like Moser, a good enough sprinter to win more than your share of the resulting finishes. With his strapping build Moser was never likely to win the one race that had eluded him: the Giro d'Italia. And the negative struggle he was locked into with Saronni, in which

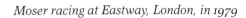
Moser racing at Eastway, London, in 1979

Francesco Moser

Moser's awesome physique

neither would permit the other to win, cannot have made the business of day-to-day racing very pleasant. If any racer looked worn, wrinkled, ready for retirement, it was Cecco when I first saw him in Flanders during the 1983 spring classics.

In cycling there is a saying that a good rider picks his parents very carefully. Cecco is the youngest of five brothers and one look at his older brother Aldo, a Grand Prix des Nations winner who was still riding at forty, and one might have seen that there was a tradition of longevity in the family. Instead, when Moser's attempt on Merckx's world hour record was announced, we all guffawed. Moser may have been, by Italian standards, the best cyclist of his generation. But he was no Merckx and Merckx's hour record, made when he was at his peak, had been far and away his proudest achievement.

That, however, was precisely the point Moser's sponsors wanted to make. It was not his superiority they wanted to demonstrate, but theirs: look what our modern scientific and technological methods can do to transform a tired war horse into the holder of the greatest of all cycling records. A gamble, it may have looked like to us on the outside, but in Moser they had, as they said, the one rider in several hundred who could respond to what they had to teach and who was susceptible to a project conducted on a truly vast national scale.

And lo and behold, here Moser was, £900,000 later, adding 1720 m (more than five 333 m laps) to Merckx's world hour record as he clocked a distance of 51.151 km. More impressive to my mind, however, than the record itself was his making the record attempt twice within a week (something he was to repeat in 1986 when he set a new sea-level record). Before Moser, everyone who had ever attempted the record had been unanimous in declaring it the most gruelling experience they had ever been through. Nor has anyone ever wanted to do it again. Yet here was Moser looking after the second, and faster, performance as if he had come in from nothing more than a tough training ride. 'It's a lot easier than riding Paris-Roubaix,' he said.

Much has been made over the technological revolution that Moser's radically redesigned bike with its moved-back rear seat and differently sized covered wheels (until then illegal) has brought into the sport. Just as substantial, to my mind, have been the wholesale changes Moser has pioneered in training methods: on the correct relation of aerobic to anaerobic work; the use of the pulse monitor; carbohydrate loading four days prior to each record attempt; and, most important of all, interval training in the hills. By the end of his preparation Moser was capable of climbing at a steady cadence in top gear an 8 km hill then riding down and doing it all over again ten times in a row. If that doesn't leave you fit . . .

With these new training methods the notion of one race preparing another has gone out of the window. When Moser won Milan-San Remo in 1984 he had not ridden a single race beforehand. And he did the same before the Giro that he won in 1984 and might have won again in 1985. What this ability to train at home will do for the season as it now stands is anybody's guess. But the ability to train at home and pick your events is bound to prolong riders' careers. One has only to note the improvement in those

Hinault in Milan-San Remo, 1983

influenced by Moser – Bontempi, Argentin, Phil Anderson – as well as Moser's 1986 sea-level world hour record, to see that the change in training methods he has pioneered is a great deal more than a passing fad.

Just as one has only to share an elevator with Merckx to feel his aura, so no matter how large one's own physical presence may be, one has only to stand next to Moser to feel very inferior. In the course of the last decade the Trentino has come to dominate Italian cycling in a way no one has since the retirement of the last *campionissimo* Felice Gimondi. To the Italians, Moser can do no wrong. To his legion of personal fans, the *tifosi*, Cecco *is* Italian cycling.

BERNARD HINAULT

One may not particularly like Bernard Hinault, but one can't help but acknowledge the pre-eminent role this darkly handsome Breton with the high cheekbones and the famous jaw has played over much of the past decade. Hinault did not go around gobbling up everything in sight in the cannibalistic manner of an Eddy Merckx. Rather he preferred to set himself goals, or as he called them, 'appointments': races that he thought he could win and often enough did win. The Tour de France was always on his

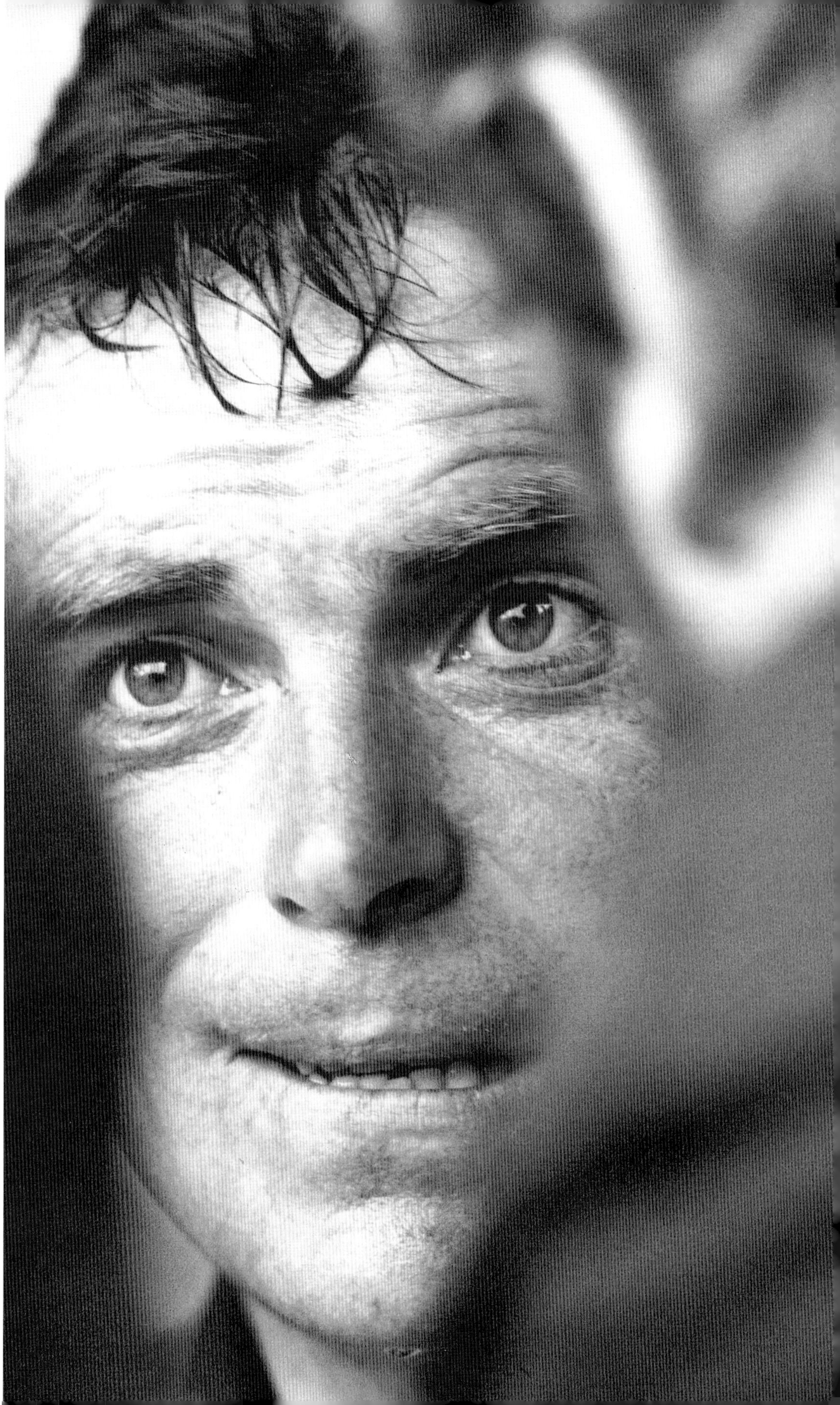

Hinault in action in the time trial that won him his first Tour de France in 1978

calendar and, between 1978 and 1986, he won the event a record-tying five times. He also won the Giro d'Italia three times, the Vuelta twice, and every major classic except Milan-San Remo and the Tour of Flanders. No one in the history of the sport has ever better disproved the notion that races are not to be won to order.

How Hinault came by his famous punctuality is hard to say. The Breton does not talk freely and has always preferred to hold what cards he has rather close to his chest. But you are not the best rider against the clock of your generation without perhaps suspecting that you do know more than the next about how to control time and tide: preparing yourself, loading up, and all the rest of it. And Hinault's vaunted time-trialling ability gave him a distinct advantage in the war of nerves a chieftain of his sort conducts with a pack. On the one hand, he could motor away on his own whenever he felt inclined; on the other, he could personally mow down anyone presumptuous enough to think he could escape on his own. He could not do this, however, day in, day out, without putting undue strains on his over-muscled legs. This is why every season he had to bring himself along so gradually, saving himself for the big ones, those he needed to keep his self-proclaimed number one standing.

Hinault comes out of a very poor rural background on the north coast of Brittany. Until recently no-one in his family has ever ridden around on anything but a bike. He didn't do well at school and was something of a loner; the sort who would like to wander around in the forest, or squat the whole of an afternoon on his haunches staring raptly at the sea. Early on he seems to have come to his abiding conviction that life is a struggle; whatever you are going to get, you are going to have to fight for. And we have seen him flailing away with his fists to get through a strikers' roadblock in Paris-Nice, or standing in the front line of the riders' strike in the 1978 Tour de France. What he likes about racing is seeing people finishing behind him; one reason he has never been tempted by a feat such as the hour record. The worse the conditions, the more he relishes the battle. His crowning achievement in this respect may well be his 9:24 victory in the 1980 Liège-Bastogne-Liège, ridden in a sub-zero blizzard. Ever since he has had no feeling in the fourth finger of his right hand.

If all this adds up, as LeMond in a heated moment of the 1986 Tour said, to an 'animal', that may well be. The badger replicas that one sees all through his house testify to something more than his hairiness: nocturnal, digging in, willing at any moment to fight, that is all very much part of his character. (His efforts to dynamite the real ones out of his fields have been a long-standing winter amusement for the French press.) And there are limits; I have seen him become enraged at the sound of a shutter clicking as he is peeing. Nor can he stand other people's fingers on his skin. Children seeking his autograph have got themselves soundly slapped for such impertinence.

This highly masculine temperament with its very definite edges makes for a natural leader; especially if one is as highly concentrated about who one is and where one is, that whole playing the game, as Hinault. Apart from the bicycle and the farm he is setting up for himself, the 'badger' has practically no interests, aside perhaps from a

facing page: Bernard Hinault
following pages, left: Francesco Moser ; right, Sean Kelly

recent hobby like stamp-collecting. But about the bicycle he is as much a fanatic as Merckx, and he may even be more inventive: there is a revolutionary quick-release pedal of his design that Look is marketing. While no slave to a training schedule –'That would make riding like working in a factory,' he says – he is equally meticulous and well-informed about training, diet (he is rumoured to have offered a doctor $35,000 to prepare him for the 1986 Tour) and all the rest that goes into a performance. His feats may be spontaneous; but they are, you may be sure, extremely well prepared. Along with this dedication comes a body hardened by years of work during his adolescence, chopping and carrying great loads of wood. While his body at 5 ft 8 ins and 140 pounds is about average, his thighs are unusually strong, a source of leverage on the moderate climbs at which he has no living peer.

To his poverty while growing up, and the suffering, the need to fight, that went with it, must be added the whole Breton ethos that has always surrounded him. If there is a people with a long tradition of suffering and exile in French history, it is the Breton – one reason they have taken road racing to their heart, to such an extent that the sport is more popular in Brittany even than in the deprived north of France. In such a climate one can see an outstanding talent like Hinault's being recognized from the start and receiving excellent coaching. What was equally important for his style of riding, depending as it does on force, the ability to turn a big gear, was that he was not over-raced. In the whole of his amateur career Hinault rode no more than 100 races; whereas another pro of the same vintage, Patrick Friou, had already logged 310 victories by the time he had turned professional.

Signed by Guimard at nineteen, Hinault did not begin winning until the spring of 1977 when he was twenty-one. His first major classic victory in Ghent-Wevelgem, when he escaped on a long solo break, could be put down to surprise – no one knew how dangerous he was. When he repeated the victory four days later in Liège-Bastogne-Liège everyone knew that a true champion had arrived. He followed this up by beating that year's Tour de France winner, Bernard Thevenet, in the Dauphiné Libéré, even though he missed a turn on a descent while leading and had to clamber back out of a ravine (the TV moment of the year), barely making it to the finish. Hinault did win the Tour on his long-awaited debut in 1978, considerably helped by Pollentier's ejection from the race. In the next four years he went on to win it three more times, the exception being 1980 when knee tendinitis forced him to withdraw at a time when he had already won four stages and held the Yellow Jersey.

Hinault may have been dominant until the first incident of knee tendinitis in 1980. Why thereafter everyone still submitted to his yoke, despite his vulnerability on steep terrain, is open to question. One would think that, with nothing to lose, they would have ganged up to attack him, rather than wait to be devoured in the time trials. We know that in a long stage race Hinault was more than a match for any single rider in a head-on challenge. But how would he have fared if subjected to a series of attacks, day after day, one mountain after the next? It is here that Hinault's machismo, 'I have prepared myself, I have announced it, here I am', along with his python-like manner of

Stephen Roche

riding (always in the front line, jaw clenched, hand never so much as deigning to drop to a gear lever) had his prey so hypnotized that only on the last uphill finish was his supremacy ever contested. And the half-minutes wrested from him in such an attack were never enough to compensate for the several-minute advantages he piled up in the long time trials.

Like many great sportsmen Hinault's domination was as much psychological as physical. 'He not only out-pedalled you,' his 1983 Vuelta runner-up Marino Lejarreta remarked, 'he out-thought you as well.' In a way this was a boss's prerogative. Once you have reached that eminence that has everybody waiting to see what you are going to do, you have them effectively in your pocket. This means you can ride a race that suits you, rather than them; one in which the rule of the bare minimum, of doing no more than you have to, can prevail. If everyone goes to sleep in the process, who cares; it's not you who invented the course.

That this thinking was largely negative may seem the shame of an era; a whole generation tricked into not racing. But then the last thing a reigning peloton boss needs is a revolt on his hands. One way or another Hinault made sure that any such rebellion, brief flare-up that it might have been, was quickly suppressed. And in his public post-race commentary Hinault made sure that the offending rebel bore the full brunt of his contempt. Didn't the fool realize that by attacking in such a manner, whole miles from the finish, he was doing himself a disservice? Didn't he want to finish on the Champs Elysées? If so, what was he doing throwing all that into jeopardy at this odd turn of the road?

Such *hauteur* does not differ markedly from what Merckx in his prime dished out. All the same one would think that some new Luis Ocana would eventually have come along to say that glory is glory; you don't enter a profession like cycling to be treated as a slave. Hinault's peasant canniness showed itself here in the way he used his public position to shape riders' attitudes. Just as the phrase, 'In our métier', with its hint of subtleties best kept from the multitudes, kept recurring whenever he spoke, so was he able to use the same suggestion of union to convince his fellow riders that the one way of bettering themselves –'We're all professionals, aren't we?'– lay in hanging on in their career as long as possible. Between 1978 and 1982, in fact, hanging on and being good might have been thought almost synonymous. Weren't the top places in the Tour going to the same riders in his day as in Merckx's: Zoetemelk, Agostinho, Van Impe? A remarkable fact, if it did not argue for a complacent mediocrity.

How Hinault would have fared in the much steeper 1983 Tour against the new attacking riding that was to surface there, we shall never know. Already in the Vuelta, two months earlier, he was very much on the ropes. That he survived had more to do with outlasting his rivals than, as Lejarreta remarked, on out-pedalling them. Even then with his inflamed knee he barely made it. And by the time he came back from his knee operation in 1984 the game had completely changed. Spirits had been liberated and they were not about to be put back in their box. To his credit Hinault caught the prevailing mood, adapting so well as to become, in the public eye, the attacker *par excellence* and popular in a way he never had been when he was unchallenged. The Tour may have come a little early for his 'never say die' tactics. By autumn he was completely restored, taking the Nations time trial handily, and going on to win the Tour of Lombardy with a breathtaking attack on the flat that saw him riding away from a whole mini-peloton.

He carried this attacking spirit into the 1985 and 1986 Tours, in both races grabbing the initiative at the first sight of the mountains in a way he never would have done earlier. Meanwhile he was stacking the deck for himself in something like his old way by buying up all the available talent. Carrera and Panasonic might be two very strong teams; La Vie Claire was definitely the All-Stars. And he probably would have succeeded in double-crossing LeMond and winning the Tour a record sixth time if he had not tried to outdo Fignon in the panache department. All the same his back-to-back Pyrenean attacks were just what the sport should be about, and the father-son internecine battle with LeMond, however crazily justified –'I'm trying to toughen him up for the future, give him character'– made for enthralling entertainment.

One may not like Hinault's character, the deviousness, the stylized 'I'm number one' posturing, the constant belittling of his opponents, or for that matter the lengths of the troughs between the brilliant, so often announced victories. All the same he has answered present with a remarkable punctuality exactly when it counted, and in his sport's own terms was undoubtedly the most successful rider of the decade. Not least remarkable is his own long-announced 'I'm not looking back' retirement in November 1986 on his thirty-second birthday, while still at the summit of his art. There is no reason to suppose that he won't equally succeed with his farm, his business association with Bernard Tapie, and all the rest of his life. There are winners in this world and Bernard Hinault is clearly one of them.

SEAN KELLY

On the bench, swivelling his body away as you approach, chary of words when not downright hostile, Sean Kelly remains for a journalist the hardest of the great riders to fathom. In an age where most of his brethren rate themselves, and are paid, according to the amount of publicity inches they have gleaned in a season, this farmer's son from Carrick-on-Suir in Tipperary remains very much the exception, closed, withdrawn, and extremely suspicious. Yet one only has to look at him joking with Stephen Roche, or know the respect with which he is held by the peloton, to see that he gets along very well without us. There may be two or three better-paid riders. There is no-one over the whole of a season who wins more often.

The one and only time I talked to Kelly was during the 1978 Tour de France when he was riding for the top rider of the mid-1970s, Freddy Maertens. Trying to get some comments out of him was only slightly easier than pulling teeth. It did not help that I knew little about himself, much less his profession. But at least the Irishman was a rider I could question without trying to make my French come out right and Kelly seemed to appreciate that I wouldn't be around long enough to plague him, so maybe he could open up a bit, a crack, without making it a habit. Then, too, my questions did not concern him personally, it was his sport, the duties of a Flandria team rider that I wanted to know about, what sort of latitude he had, how did he chase? (Kelly,

Sean Kelly

A competitor's usual view of Sean Kelly – from behind!

characteristically, was for letting them hang in the wind; teach those trying to break away a lesson!) As we talked I gathered the awe in which he held Maertens: 'When I tried once to follow Freddy on his 56 x 12 my legs ached for a week.'

Our chat could not have been draining. A few hours later, as part of his guard dog duties, Kelly found himself in a break powered by Bruyère and Knetemann, and ended up winning the stage for his first Tour victory. Carried away, I wrote how becoming the 'Kelly'-green jersey would look on this Irishman's shoulders. That, too, was to come to pass.

The 1978 Tour would have other consequences for Kelly as well. When Pollentier and Maertens fell out as a direct result of it the Irishman found himself badly wanted by both of them. Flattering, one can imagine, to anyone else, all that public acrimony; to Kelly it meant that he was being propelled out of the nest sooner than he was ready for it. In choosing Pollentier's Splendor over Maertens and Flandria's French affiliate De Gribaldy (who had discovered Kelly), the Irishman made a sensible choice. He was being paid more and he was being offered more scope as a quasi-team leader. He could not have foreseen that, like many a new organization assembled from scratch out of the whims of a millionaire, Splendor was to have all sorts of trouble getting its back-up material together: bikes that wouldn't break; tyres that wouldn't pop. He would also find that Splendor had too many ambitious riders, among them such excellent sprinters as Eddy Planckaert and Guido Van Calster. Some people can do business on the committee system; others find that life is only fun when you are running the show. In Kelly's case it was to mean working for the collection of underpaid hasbeens that De Gribaldy habitually assembled. But a smaller, less pretentious team can have its advantages for a rider of Kelly's sort. When you don't have to compete for a team's loyalty you can concentrate on winning races, and that's exactly what Kelly proceeded to do.

Before returning to De Gribaldy in 1982 Kelly had been for the five years of his professional life, a fourth place in the 1980 Vuelta aside, strictly a sprinter. It gave him a mask, and a glamorous, highly paid one at that, especially in the context of Belgian racing. But like all masks it tended to be confining. Before becoming a professional he had shown signs of being able to bend a more fully strung bow. You are not Irish national time trial champion on an 80 km course at nineteen without proving you have much of the equipment needed to win stage races. That same year in the Milk Race he likewise showed he could climb with the best; a talent he more than confirmed a year later in winning the 1976 amateur Tour of Lombardy. It was this all-round performer that De Gribaldy wanted as his team leader.

Over the winter Kelly trained harder than he ever had. His form was such that he not only won the hilly season-opening Tour du Haut Var, but to everyone's astonishment followed it up by taking Paris-Nice, winning four stages in the process. Of these it was the last, the hill climb of the Col d'Eze time trial, which he won by 44 seconds from race leader Gilbert Duclos-Lassalle, that marked the turning point in

Kelly, seen here on the Joux-Plane pass, has a great fear of the big mountains in the Tour de France

Kelly's career. From then on there was nothing, the Tour de France perhaps aside, he could not theoretically win. A new cannibal was launched.

I remember seeing Kelly on the podium after the Goodwood world championships in which he finished third behind Guiseppe Saronni and Greg LeMond after being the strongest presence of the race. Voluble, answering questions at length in Flemish, French, English, here was someone clearly transformed by what he had begun to achieve. At the end of the year he capped it all by getting married to his hometown sweetheart, Linda, for an Irishman never the lightest of steps.

There was every indication that 1983 was to be the year in which Kelly would do everything, including wiping out Hinault in the Tour de France. I watched him win Paris-Nice and the manner of it, from the beginning of the race to the end, could not have been more impressive. But unfortunately during the Tour des Midi-Pyrenées soon afterwards he fell heavily at a feed on an awkwardly placed downhill incline, fracturing his collar bone. Another rider would have been out for four months at least. Kelly was racing two months later and his recovery was such that he even won the eleven-day mid-June Tour of Switzerland ahead of LeMond. As far as the forthcoming Tour de France went, that *was* asking a bit much and Sean did not exactly distinguish himself (despite the most amazing last mountain recoveries). But to a Kelly a race, big or little, is like a ship to a pirate. One can imagine the temptations of a stage race in Switzerland that was the richest in cycling.

Such inclinations meant that while Kelly won a great many races, fifteen in 1982, sixteen, despite his broken collar bone, the following year, he had never in his six years of racing won a classic. Was it timidity, as De Gribaldy suggested? Or an even more basic failure of intelligence to anticipate and react fast enough when confronted with so many unknowns, whereas in a stage race you soon get to know what to expect? Kelly's winning of the Tour of Lombardy at the end of 1983 from a highly motivated LeMond broke a last psychological barrier. He followed it up in 1984 by winning just about everything, thirty-three races in all, including the two hardest spring classics, Paris-Roubaix and Liège-Bastogne-Liège. His early season dominance with fifteen victories had an awed LeMond declaring, 'Kelly is a full twenty per cent better than any of the rest of us.'

Can one rider so eclipse everyone else? Was Kelly another blood doper *à la* Fignon? At any rate 1985 witnessed a marked falling off in the number and quality of Kelly's victories. Then at the beginning of October came the Nissan Tour of Ireland. Whoosh, a chance to ride before his countrymen, and Kelly's morale was restored. He went on to win the Tour of Lombardy and with it the Pernod best rider of the year trophy.

It is customary to talk about Kelly as a quintessentially Irish rider. And as Kelly's remarkable October turnabout suggests, Ireland has everything to do with his morale. (This Irish background is admirably covered in David Walsh's biography.) For my part, though, I think it helps place Kelly better as a cyclist to see him as the last of the Flemish riders. This is a title usually associated with the post-war rider, Brik Schotte, who has become appropriately enough the man in day-to-day charge of the De Gribaldy teams. As exemplified by Schotte it stood for a certain type of mentality: poor, willing to suffer, narrowly focussed, and hard, hard, hard.

Kelly had all this in him from his Irish small farm background: the outside loo; the dogs that have to be chained before you can step from your car; the one career possible, as a bricklayer on a construction site, stretching away and away into the grey mists. On the positive side, along with the self-reliance, came a physical strength that even by peasant standards is impressive. Kelly may not look like a rider, and his pedalling style still suffers from the effects of learning to race on a bike too small for him. But he is probably as strong pound for pound as any rider in the peloton. And in a profession of iron wills there is no one harder. Kelly never has a bad word to say about anybody and, even more amazing, never seems to need anything from his team.

In coming to Belgium as a foreign mercenary this Irishman stepped into a waiting tradition: the little flat-roofed brick houses; the pride in craftmanship; a tendency to value one another by their humour, their practical jokes. How well Kelly adapted may be seen in that when I met him he spoke English with a Flemish accent. His habits, from his insistence on going to bed at nine to his frugality, could not be more Flemish. Until 1985 he rented rooms in the incomparably grimy Brussels suburb of Vilvoorde. He drives a five-year-old Citroen, still clamps his own bike to the car's bike rack, and to this day even washes his own shorts. As for the style of racing he has adopted, one has only to compare him with Stephen Roche with his Celtic mercuriality, his insistence on flair, 'nose', sniffing out the right break. There is, after all, an Irish style.

For a Flemish rider cycling is not so much a sport as a profession. Where livelihoods are concerned money counts; why waste your time riding in a race you can't win? In coming to Belgium Kelly not only received an incomparable initiation into the sport from the bottom up, he also learned how to deal; maybe not in the league of a master like Jan Raas, but sufficiently up there. Much of the respect in which he is held in the peloton has to do with the strength of his word; what he promises, he delivers. There is no better example of Kelly's astuteness than the sequence of deals Walsh traces – in effect, a trade of Blois-Chaville for Kwantum team support in the Tour of Lombardy – which won him the 1985 Pernod trophy.

With the victories and the money and the backing Kelly's confidence has grown. No longer do classics like Milan-San Remo slip away from him. And the level of the teamwork he can command is beginning to reach Maertens-like proportions. In a sprint it is Kelly who invariably dictates the terms. He may never be quite the cannibal Merckx was, winning everything every possible way. But season in, season out, he will win more than any other cyclist. As a cyclist and a man he has come in a few years a very long way. To the rest of us it is highly satisfactory to see the blood of an ancient tradition flowing so strongly through these new Irish veins.

STEPHEN ROCHE

On a bike hunched forward like a small tiger, with his unmistakable Celtic combination of black wavy hair, white skin and cornflower blue eyes, Stephen Roche is instantly recognizable. 'The Dublin Smiler', one trade journal called him fittingly. In talking to Stephen you can't help but be struck by the tone of pride that radiates out over the whole of his life. Not everyone thinks of Dundrum, the working-class South Dublin

Roche awaiting the start of the Grand Prix des Nations time trial

Stephen Roche time-trialling in Paris-Nice, 1985

suburb he hails from, as paradise. To Stephen that's what it is, flanked by a sea you can swim in every day of the year on one side and the waterfalls and forests of the Wicklow Hills (where Stephen dreams of building a small house one day) on the other. Various people may have set their feet in paradise at one time or another. Stephen is the only person I have ever met who can give the impression of never having left it. I remember once mentioning this to Phil Anderson. 'You're right,' the Aussie replied, 'whenever I'm depressed all I have to do is go over and talk to Stephen and I'm instantly cheered up.'

Most riders act as if the decisions of a race were entirely instinctive; get your body in shape and your experience will take care of the rest. For Stephen races are won just as much with the head as with the legs. In talking to him this emphasis on using one's head, on the necessity of guile, comes up again and again. But by thinking Roche means something more than the poker game tactics, the art of the bluff cultivated by a Hinault or a Phil Anderson. Hinault and Anderson are riders who can, on occasion, sprint. As such they can afford to wait. Whereas Stephen is a rider condemned for lack of a sprint to attack, an always risky proposition. That's one reason why you always see Stephen up front in a race, ready, waiting. And it's where his natural positiveness comes in. For him attacking is not the impossible thing everyone claims it is. You just have to know how, when. On the subject there is no more lucid informant.

'You're so often in the winning break,' I ask him soon after we first met, as we are driving out to see the property on which he is about to start building in the Oise valley, an hour to the north of Paris, 'since you can't go with them all, how do you know what's the right wagon?' 'The nose,' Stephen answers, obviously giving nothing away, 'I smell them out.' No matter how often I return to the question, there is always this tactical 'nose' that one has to imagine in a race, doggedly sniffing about. I know there is more to it than a hunch, that it's been preceded by all that sizing up of one's rivals that goes on in the first part of a stage race, trying to figure out who will have to be marked, who anticipated. But just as a writer who depends on rhythm hears experience, that dry hillside curving above in a bush of words, so a rider has to make use of evidence from senses other than his eyes. A crash is not something a rider ever sees, it's a sound and it's by its distinctness he knows whether he is in the middle of it or not.

It may be my frustration that moves Stephen to explain, as we approach the top of a small rare hummock, something of his attacking strategy. 'I like to have a go just before the top of a hill, that moment when you hear everyone behind changing down. If you have ten yards before the top it can look like a hundred on the descent. And as soon as a gap is made you have a chance.'

'Do you look around,' I ask, 'check the gap you have created?' (Most riders are constantly turning around, even in the last yards of a sprint.)

'I just go – with my head down. After some three miles I'll turn around and see if anyone is with me. If they are, I'll start trying to organize them so we relay one another. If I've not made the break myself, of course it's a whole other matter,' he adds with a wink. 'Then you've got to try to work less than the next fellow. When taking a relay, I like to sprint into the lead and then drop off quickly, thus forcing the person following me in the rotation to tire himself out making up the gap. Tricks of the trade,' Stephen adds with an apologetic smile.

Jostein Willmann and Stephen Roche during Liège-Bastogne-Liège

'How about the wind here when you train?' I ask, seeing nothing in the way of a brake in this rich, wheat-growing landscape.

'Wherever you ride there is wind, coming from one angle or another. You have to be able to take advantage of each quirk it offers. Zoetemelk, a rider of limited means, has that ability. So does Kuiper. Whenever an echelon forms they are always in it.'

Stephen's admiration of good technical riders such as Zoetemelk and Kuiper shows in the meticulousness with which he prepares a time trial, far and away his favourite event. Everything has been calculated, from the bike which will have taken over a year to get right, down to the amount of fluid in his bidon. At times one feels he shaves things a bit too close. I remember a time trial in the Tour de France in 1984 where, after leading most of the way, he simply ran out of fuel. As it turned out his bidon contained only 300 cc of liquid as against the winner Fignon's 1000 cc. Most riders like to finish a time trial with something left, so they can dismount on their own. Not Stephen, he wants to go down to the limit, and if they don't have to lift him off his bike at the end he hasn't ridden a satisfactory time trial. His courage, allied to the smoothest of pedalling styles, couldn't be more admirable. But it does make you shudder.

I have mentioned Stephen's pride in his life and what he has accomplished: 'Everything I've got I've earned.' There's considerable strength in such a statement; but it can also mean that he is often out on a limb of his own with no means of summoning assistance. With Peugeot he was often complaining of the lack of support, 'I never saw one of them all day – were they racing?' At the other end of the scale he would set such a pace in a team time trial that in the first few kilometres a third of the team was dropped. For a would-be leader there is an art in using team-mates rather than cutting yourself off from them. At Peugeot he had a natural ally in Phil Anderson and they made between them a very effective combination. But though they respected one another highly, and had a lot in common, they were not in any sense friends. Partly this was a question of class. Stephen could never understand Phil blowing what little money he had on a white Mercedes with a 200 kmph cruising speed. And he disapproved of the way in which Phil's American wife Anne would turn up now and then at a race. 'You don't bring your wife to the factory, do you?' Not that Stephen could not bend with the prevailing wind, pleased to have Lydia at his side in the 1983 world championships. But behind Stephen's geniality, the twinkle in the eye, the ready smile, there is something that can turn sour very fast. In cycling he will always be a bit of a lone wolf; able to lead, but not always to command.

In view of Stephen's occasional breakdowns over the years – often problems of skin, boils, etc – doubts have been cast as to whether someone so finely tuned is strong enough to win the Tour de France. Admittedly Stephen does not have the physique of a LeMond or a Kelly. But some of this apparent lack of strength may be deceptive. From eight onwards Stephen carried milk bottles, three on each arm, up four or five flights of tenement stairs for the pleasure of being with his father on his rounds. And he takes his ability to withstand extraordinary cold from his father, a security officer now, who swims every day of the year in the Irish Sea (Stephen with his Irish skin fares less well in the heat, and it may keep him from winning a midsummer event like the Tour de France.) His closeness to his father, who had ridden well in his youth, may have acted as a hidden incentive in his taking up bike racing.

But his parents didn't do much to encourage his racing. When Stephen began it was on a bike with fat 'wired-on' tyres borrowed from a friend; a machine so antiquated that a special category could be created for him. After a second year racing on a red and blue bike held together with borrowed parts, Roche plunked out £60 of his own hard-earned money for a Mercier frame that he was to ride for the next four years and which he still owns. He built the bike in a day on the eve of the junior national championships and did well enough to come in third.

Though Stephen went, as he says, 'up the amateur ladder like a light', he received no sponsorship until his last two years before going to France. Even then he was training at night after work. His father had insisted – with complete justification, Stephen feels – that he finish his four-year apprenticeship as an automotive welder before trying his luck as a rider. Then, too, Stephen really liked everything about the work from the stripping down and welding of engines to the feel of the oil on his clothes.

Most riders when they switch teams bring along a personal *domestique,* a masseur. Stephen brought along from Peugeot to La Redoute his French mechanic, Patrick Valcke. For Stephen, as for few riders, the bicycle is 'la petite reine'.

In Ireland word travels fast and Roche's victory in Ireland's national tour, the Ras Tailteann, earned him a place on the national team. But he soon fell out with his coach over the amount of training mileage being required. As he says, 'The reason why no one between Sean and me ever did anything isn't lack of talent. They were getting themselves burnt out at an age when their bodies were still growing.' Roche could see a first-hand example of this in Irish international Kevin Reilly, who was to marry Roche's older sister. For Stephen training, and it's part of what makes him such a good time triallist, is a matter of knowing how to listen to what your body is telling you. 'I never ride further than I want to. The same', he adds, 'goes for what I eat.'

Before dropping out of the national team Roche had met and impressed the French national team coach Lucien Bailly. It was through Bailly that he received an invitation from the Peugeot sponsored ACBB to ride for them while preparing for the Moscow Olympics. On 11 February 1980, the day after he received his machinist's degree, he flew to Paris. The rightness of having a trade to fall back on is something Stephen in conversation keeps returning to. For a Greg LeMond, a Phil Anderson, cycle racing can carry the allure of a sport. For this working-class Dubliner it is definitely a profession.

In going to ride for the ACBB Stephen approached it as he would have approached any trade apprenticeship. He was there to learn and anything they exacted of him, no matter how humiliating, was part and parcel of the learning process. An English club-mate remembers being impressed by his 'will to succeed. It was written all over his face. He was willing to do anything they asked of him, from cleaning shoes to riding his eyeballs out to close down a gap.'

Stephen came to grips with the language in the same positive spirit. He had never studied French at school, but he has a natural ear – he plays the accordion – and approached it as one might a new sound system. 'You just have to realise that each letter of the alphabet has a different sound from what it is in English.' While Stephen still has trouble writing the language ('Just enough to fill in a cheque'), his speech was soon virtually accentless.

Roche does not find his top form, he says, as quickly as some riders do. But once he finds it, it stays with him without the ups and downs, the need to 'peak', that most riders experience. By mid-April he was winning races, the Route de France, the amateur Paris-Roubaix. He went on from there, never losing a time trial, to succeed Graham Jones and Robert Millar as the overall French amateur points champion. At the end of the year he became one more in Peugeot's growing stable of English-speaking riders.

It's one thing to turn pro; it's another, because of the different style of riding the longer distances demand, to start winning races. It's safe to say that no one in the history of the sport ever arrived with a bigger bang than did this twenty-one-year-old Irishman in 1981, pocketing the Tour of Corsica and Paris-Nice as if born to it. He went on from there to win the Tour de l'Indre-et-Loire and the autumn Etoile des Espoirs, while most impressive of all placing second behind Hinault in the Grand Prix des Nations time trial. Why the pack let him and Bossis, two Peugeots, get away in a break of four during the Corsican Tour is something Roche still finds hard to fathom. So confident was the much faster Bossis of winning the overall race that he let Stephen win the stage sprint for his first professional victory. Instead it was Roche who won the overall event. He went on from there to wrest the race lead from Dutch first year pro Adri Van der Poel on the penultimate stage of Paris-Nice; an advantage he would more than confirm by winning the Col d'Eze time trial.

After such a fabulous season there were many who picked Roche as Hinault's principal rival in the forthcoming Tour de France, despite his being as yet untested in the mountains. Instead Stephen's 1982 season was a considerable let-down. 'I could hang on,' he told me, 'but I lacked punch where it counted in the last two hundred yards.' Even more telling, from Stephen's point of view, was that never once did he finish in the first ten in a time trial. Not that this kept him from performances that any other young rider would have cherished: a gutsy second behind Jan Raas in a snow-doused Amstel Gold Race, followed a few days later by a third in the Dunkirk Four Days.

Was Roche's another case of too much too soon, one more young rider who had let himself be ridden into the ground? There were a few who had detected the first warning signs when Stephen pulled out of the June Dauphiné, complaining of a general fatigue. 'I'm too young to ride the Tour de France as my sports director De Muer wants me to,' he had said at the time. (Of course, one can see De Muer's point of view; when a rider is going that well it's hard to get him to stop.) When I saw Stephen after the 1982 Trophée des Grimpeurs, ridden a few miles from the Seine barge-town of Conflans where he was then living in a converted attic apartment, he was complaining of the same general pain as a year earlier. 'Only now it's not only my legs and back, it's my arms as well. I just don't know what's wrong. Fortunately I'm to go to the cardiological institute in Cologne next week to be tested.' Health, of course, is something you don't know you have until you lose it. It looked to me as if Stephen might have strained his heart in starting off with such a splash.

I am not sure what damage the tests revealed, but when I saw the Peugeot publicity director René Beillon two months later he said that the signs of angina we had feared were not permanent and would probably disappear if Stephen went home to Dublin and took a complete rest. One may wonder what a 'complete rest' entails. In any other sport an athlete of Stephen's potential would probably have been granted the rest of the year off. But cycling is a sport where a rider is paid to be seen – on a bike, racing – and Stephen was back with Peugeot in mid-August, training seven hours a day so as to be fit enough to help his Irish team-mate and best friend, Sean Kelly, try to win the Goodwood world championships.

Stephen's autumn season, his services to Kelly aside, was far from brilliant. But the mysterious pains were gone and Stephen felt he knew where he had erred in his 1982 pre-season training. For 1983 he was determined to come in fit. When in January new Peugeot manager Roland Berland asked him to list what stage races he wanted to ride Stephen refused to commit himself beyond the Mediterranean Tour and Paris-Nice.

Robert Millar

'How', Berland stormed, 'do you expect me to plan a season?' For Stephen it was a way of underlining his need to take stock. 'My 3000 mile check-up', I remember his calling it on the 'phone.

Though there were a few set-backs – on the Ventoux in Paris-Nice and a few days later when he had to drop out with a weather-aggravated knee strain – Roche passed his check-up points better than expected. Already in February he was pulling gears he could not have pulled a year earlier and placing high in the time trials. By the end of April he was winning races, the Tour de Wallonie and a not very hilly Tour de Romandie with considerable help from Phil Anderson. And Anderson and Roche, both attackers, made between them a rather formidable pair. The way the two of them bested four Renault riders in the concluding stage of Paris-Bourges (eliminating them one by one, until there was only one left pincered between them) was for *L'Équipe* correspondent Jean-Jacques Simmler the finest example of tactical riding he had seen in years.

Even more important for Roche's future was his dramatic improvement as a climber. At the beginning of the season I remember him speaking admiringly of LeMond, using the term 'ballader' to describe the effortlessness with which the American climbed. As for himself he had no idea which was better – sitting or standing up or, more likely, a combination of the two. A few weeks later, on the Ventoux, he found himself dropped and struggling. But climbing is, as Van Impe has remarked, an art that can be learned. And in the course of rubbing shoulders with the best climbers in the world on the Tour de France Roche made startling progress, finishing second to Van Impe on the Avoriaz time trial, then capping it with an even more remarkable ascent of the Joux-Plane side by side with Robert Millar that saw them first at the summit. From that moment on Roche could go to virtually any team he wanted.

In the next months the offers poured in. From Hinault, who had not yet hit on the rather more expensive LeMond alternative; from his former Peugeot director De Muer who with Geminiani had been asked to take over at La Redoute; from Peugeot, loath to lose a leader who knew the system from the inside out. For Stephen it was not an easy decision to make, as the two contracts he signed – and had to go to court over – made clear. In the end he chose La Redoute because it offered him the opportunity to be his own man. 'At Peugeot', he told me, 'I would always have been an apprentice, never a true leader. I wouldn't mind riding for them later on, but for them to respect me I have got to go away.' Roche was to remain with La Redoute, despite several tempting offers, until 1985 when the team finally folded. By then he was riding well enough to be able to transfer to Visentini's Carrera for a reputed salary of £200,000 a year. Shortly thereafter the Irishman took a spectacular fall in the Paris Six Day when a tyre blew out. The resulting knee injury was seriously to compromise his 1986 season.

If his knees hold up, and the rumoured Ice Age we are in does not suddenly recoil (Stephen like many Irishmen does not tolerate heat well), Roche should successfully challenge LeMond and Fignon in future Tours de France. He can time-trial and climb as well as either, and as a master of tactics there is no one better. With his willingness to attack he is bound to bring excitement to any race he rides.

Phil Anderson

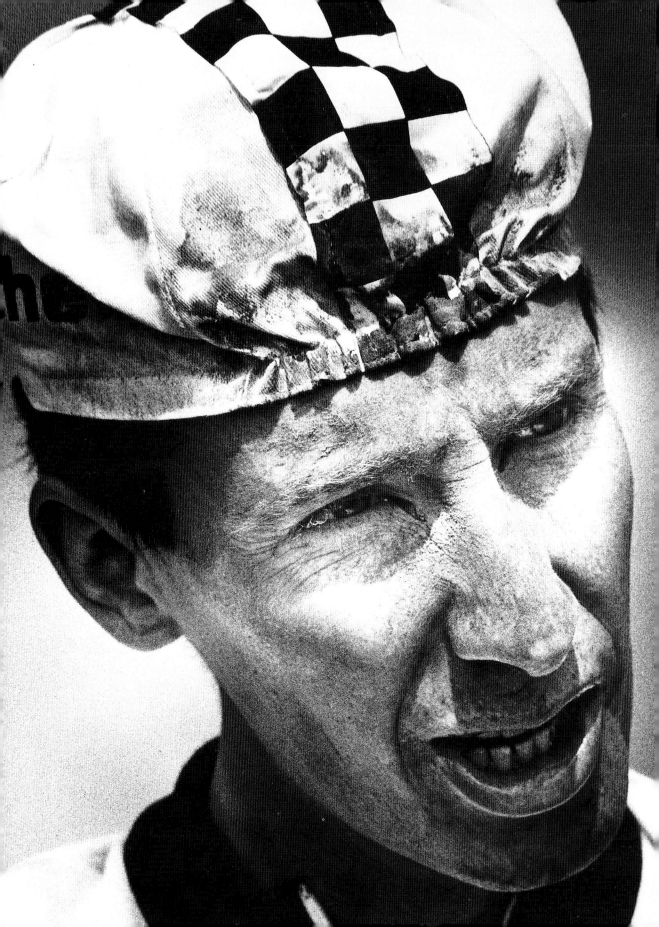

ROBERT MILLAR

The first thing that strikes you about Robert Millar is his size. With his distinctive pointy nose he looks more like a Dickensian chimney-sweep than a man who makes his living out in the wind of a road. I remember while once in Robert's native Glasgow hearing his friend and mentor, Billy Bilsland, a good rider of the Simpson-Hoban-Wright generation, say, 'Millar's whole body isn't as big as one of Sean Kelly's thighs.' A few months later, after the Scot's great stage victory at Luchon, there was a Tour de France director describing him in his editorial as the *asticot* of the pack. 'What is an *asticot*?' I asked Robert. 'Eugh,' he replied, making a face, 'one of those things you use in fishing. I think we call them maggots. Then,' he said, suddenly recognizing the parallel, 'there are the blue-eyed ones.'

'Maggot' may be a bit cruel, but the impression sticks. At 5ft 6ins Millar is the same size as 1976 Tour winner Lucien Van Impe, a resemblance that Millar takes care to emphasize. But where Van Impe glows with good humour and every appearance of health there is something decidedly reticent, not to say sour, about this Glaswegian. Partly it's the way he speaks, in a voice that struggles to rise above a whisper. Partly, it's Glasgow. When you're born in the Gorbals, which has some claim to be the worst slum in Europe, you may not flow with the milk of human kindness. And you may have a right to feel haunted. If it wasn't somebody else, it could have been you: there behind bars, if not dead at fifteen. As Millar puts it, summarizing the lessons of this urban jungle, 'Fellow who can't climb up tree fast enough gets eaten.' Substitute 'hill' for 'tree' and one might suddenly see a whole vocation blossom.

The city itself Millar detests and, despite a father and friends who care deeply about him, he has kept his visits back to a minimum. Partly it's the weather; 'Disgusting!', as he says, "Know any place else where it rains during the day, but not at night? I like the people, not the place, grey, grey, grey. But remember I spent the first five years of my life in the Gorbals before moving to Pollok on the city outskirts – a modern housing estate built on a razed slum and fast turning back into one. Everybody there works for the same factory. I worked there too.' One can see how the revenge that is crime might have beckoned to young Millar. 'If you get nicked, don't they feed you?' he said, summing up the prevailing attitude. When I asked him what made him take up cycle racing, he replied, 'To stay out of trouble. Once you stop school there's nothing to do. I had the A and O levels to have gone to university. For what – an engineering degree? Like my Dad, they're all on the dole.'

For this dead-end kid nature, a shrub, a flower, would have seemed utterly exotic. Asked his impressions of 'green', he remembers it as where you went to lie down in, 'on a summer's day'. Cycling became, like fishing, a means of escaping the city; an escape made easy by the hills and quiet roads that are to be reached within a few minutes of Glasgow. Gradually, as he cycled about, he became more and more involved with nature, the different smells, the warm air and where it lies. And this made him

Robert Millar

conscious in turn of what he was eating. 'For a year and a half,' he said, 'I was a vegetarian, a fish vegetarian. Now I eat white meat as well.'

When he came to France at the age of twenty, after winning the British amateur title for the first time, it was with the intention of making a clean break. But the country itself was no bouquet of roses and Millar still recoils from the culture shock of his first week when he felt completely lost. And he never cottoned on to Boulogne-Billancourt, the west Paris industrial suburb where his riding club, the Peugeot-sponsored ACBB, was based. 'Just like Glasgow,' he observed, 'except in August when the city's half deserted.' But unlike Scotland there were people on the road cheering when he raced and he got off on the right wheel by winning his first race, in a bunch sprint no less. He went on to win thirteen victories and the Spidel and Merlin Plage awards as France's best overall amateur. In the Valkenburg (Holland) world championships in 1979 Millar instigated the decisive four-man break and might well have won the gold medal if he had not pulled out of his toe clips during the final sprint; a showing that prompted *Sunday Times* reporter John Wilcockson in a New Year's article to predict that here was a British unknown who might one year win the Tour de France.

Peugeot signed him after the Worlds and saw fit to keep him for three years despite the fact that he did not win a single race. The transition from amateur to professional is rarely easy, even if, like Millar, you have had the results to be able to enter by the front door. One would think that Millar's build and climbing ability would have made him an automatic choice for the Tour de France; but the Scot was never allowed to ride it. During the first two of these years the charge that he was too young and not strong enough might have applied. By 1982, however, he was ready and with a chance to double his salary through the post-Tour criteriums he was more than willing to do whatever service his team leader Bernaudeau required to justify his selection.

After Millar's good seventh place in the first climbers' stage race, the Tour de Romandie, his manager De Muer announced that it would be a two-man contest between the Scot and retiring veteran André Chalmel to see who would ride the Tour. With Chalmel debilitated by the effects of his horrid crash in the end of May Bordeaux-Paris and Millar toughening himself up with post-race rides of 100 km there would seem to have been no choice, especially as Bernaudeau wanted Millar. But a contest between a popular veteran like Chalmel who is president of the riders' union and a young foreign mercenary like Millar is never going to be decided on a purely athletic basis. De Muer had never got on with Millar. Now that he was about to retire he decided, no doubt wisely, to toss Chalmel a last bone. Meanwhile Robert was so certain that he would be picked that he had already said good-bye to everyone he would not be seeing for the next month and a half when he read in the papers of Chalmel's selection. 'What they did to me,' he commented with some emphasis, 'you wouldn't do to a dog.'

That left Millar with no choice than to salvage his season with a good ride in the Tour de l'Avenir. Greg LeMond was in a class of his own – he won by ten minutes – but Millar's second place brought its satisfactions and he renewed his contract with Peugeot for a substantial boost in salary. 'At least you know they aren't going to throw in the towel in mid-season like Van Impe's team last year.'

'Does that mean you get to ride the Tour next year?' I asked.

'Not in the least. My Avenir ride helps, but I've still got to earn my place.'

'How can you be expected to do well in the mountains, if you have to do a lot of team work as well?' I asked, voicing a common complaint.

'Ask Pollentier,' Millar snapped back. 'If you're chasing down everything that moves you may find yourself latching onto a good wagon. Still you are limited because you are not allowed to contribute and no one likes towing a dead fish to the finish, only to have it suddenly revive.'

'What happens if you see an opportunity and go away on your own?' I asked.

'You had better win. Even then you are going to have some team-mates sore at you. The last rap anyone wants is to be known as a bloody individualist.'

'You seem to like being a domestique,' I said, 'May I ask why?'

'The money. We all like defending a lead and working for someone because we have a chance to earn something. There's not much you can earn sitting on your backside at home.'

'Do you train while you're here?' I asked. 'Yates tells me he is doing three to four hours a day.'

'That's because his season begins in February and ends about the first of May. I'm just coming into form in May. I could, I suppose, ride Paris-Nice, but I don't like all that cold and wet.'

'But you're from Glasgow, you ought to be inured to all this . . .'

'Greyness?' Millar interjected.

I asked Millar about climbing, a subject on which he is one of the world's leading authorities. Warming to his subject, he described Anderson's mistake in taking Beat Breu's wheel at the bottom of a hill in the 1982 Tour and as a consequence blowing up, unable to match a true climber's irregular rhythm. For himself he preferred not to get caught up in the rush to the front at the beginning of a climb. Better to take things more slowly, find your rhythm, and from there proceed. On the outside of a little group, preferably, where there is more air . . . As we talked about the differences between climbers, those who climbed on the odd as against the even chain ring, the sharing of bidons, 'you never know when you are going to be stranded', he kept stressing his limitations, his inability to take the wheel of a Bernaudeau on a descent, his hatred of the rough stuff involved in just staying up front, let alone participating in a mass sprint finish. But despite the contentment he kept emphasizing, of someone who had found his niche, one that would keep him employed until his mid-thirties, there was a sense that there were hidden fires underneath and that a more complete rider was waiting to be let out.

I saw Millar again in the Seillans training camp a few months later; a Millar more like his 'won't give you the time of day' legend; refusing even to acknowledge before his team-mates that we had ever met. Against the chauvinist background then prevailing such an expression of insecurity was understandable. The better riders may have been, like Roche and Anderson, English-speaking. And with Peiper and Yates unable to speak French they did form a definite group. But the French held the ultimate power and Millar's loyalties were very much more with his fellow climber and best friend, Pascal Simon, near whom he had moved (outside Troyes in eastern Champagne). In acknowledging and perhaps talking to an English-speaking journalist he would have been endangering this solidarity that he had very carefully built up.

I saw Millar a few times more later that spring; on the Dauphiné where he, Simon and Anderson out-manoeuvred a tactically naive LeMond; during the Midi Libre as he and Roche were preparing themselves for the coming Tour with post-race 100 km rides. And I was there by his cot with John Wilcockson the morning after his superb attacking victory at Pau-Luchon as he told us how he had anticipated Arnaud's attack on the descent of the Soulor hill, how he had persuaded the Colombian to work with him, and his fears as he turned around and saw Delgado overtaking him on the final descent. He was very happy, it was his first victory after four years as a professional, and a memorable one at that. On the strength of it he was telling us how he was going to wrest away Laurent Fignon's White Jersey as the best neo-pro. He had the stages all figured out, A,B,C,D, so many minutes on this climb, so many on that time-trial. All this, of course, was not to be, but we did see the Scot and Roche breast the last real climb of the Tour, the Joux-Plane, side by side, and it was clear that Millar's encouraging presence had a lot to do with Stephen's sudden tranformation into someone who could more than hold his own on a substantial Tour climb.

Millar confirmed his class with another Pyrenean victory a year later at Pla d'Adet (just about the only mountain stage Fignon did not win). By 1985 he had progressed sufficiently to have become Peugeot's leader in stage races. Peugeot entered the Vuelta with the thought that its mountains might give him a springboard, and the Scot confirmed by winning several stages and riding a faultless race. That he was screwed out of the final victory may have had as much to do with his own naiveness as with his manager Berland's ineptitude. But to have stood up so successfully to the demands of such a long grind meant that he had every right to be considered one of the foremost candidates to win the Tour de France.

The Scot's other actions showed the extent of his new ambitions. He moved to Flemish Belgium because it was the best way, as he saw it, of improving himself as an all-round rider. And with his customary thoroughness he taught himself Flemish. He also started to work out in a gym, building himself up so that he could time-trial more effectively. At the end of the 1985 season, with winning the Tour de France in mind, he signed a substantial contract with Panasonic, thus assuring himself the best possible back-up. In the three seasons since I had met him in Glasgow he had come a very long way.

How much further Millar can go with his physical limitations is a matter of some debate. John Wilcockson has written about chatting with Stephen Roche in a café as the 1986 Tour prepared to approach the mountains and seeing the Irishman turn and point to Millar as he stepped through the door, 'There goes the 1986 Tour winner.' But when the chips came down, in a signally brutal Tour, the Scot proved simply not strong enough. There are many reasons given on Millar's behalf, from all the chasing of the La Vie Claires he had to do to the bronchitis that eventually led to his withdrawal. But there are a growing number who think that Millar will have to give up Paris-Nice and the Vuelta and instead, like Van Impe, build his season around doing well in a single event, the Tour de France. There are many who feel that he does not eat enough of the

An anxious Robert Millar before the 20th stage of the 1986 Tour of Spain

right sort of food; you can't get through an extended season on a dict of cakes. There is also the question, voiced by Hinault, of whether Millar's new time-trialling prowess has not been gained at the expense of his efficacy as a climber; you may be more powerful, but you still have to carry those new muscles. On the other hand, it may simply take a while for your body to adjust to its new possibilities. Millar is an intelligent and supremely dedicated sportsman. It is hard to believe that he will let a matter of diet, or anything else for that matter, get in the way of those Tour de France heights he has obviously set for himself.

PHIL ANDERSON

It is the 1984 Tour de France at L'Alpe d'Huez. Phil Anderson has just pedalled in, seven minutes behind the stage winner, Luis Herrera. Even if the pain in his chest is not what it was an hour earlier when he thought he was going to die, he looks remarkably shattered. A difficult moment to accost a cyclist, especially one with Phil's stake in the Tour, but there is one of us up to the demands of the profession who sticks out his mike and asks, 'Phil, is this the worst day of your life?' Anderson looks him over, pauses, then decides to enlighten him about the sport: 'Every day, you know, is hard. It's the good days that are so rare.'

Of the same quality is Sean Kelly's tribute: 'Phil Anderson is the only rider I know who attacks even when he is hurting.' Anderson himself might put such attacks down to the need to 'bluff', an ability he admires in Hinault. But Phil does not have anything like Hinault's cards at his disposal. As a rider he is more of a thrasher than the beautifully synchronized pedalling machine that Hinault is. And he is big at 6 ft tall to be doing what he likes best – climbing. But if you want a charismatic leader to build a team around you could do worse than start with this rangy Australian with the instantly recognizable crew-cut hair and lean, wolf-like cast of face. As Kelly says, his courage is unique; he doesn't know what it is to give up. And his presence makes any race exciting, because he is willing to put himself at any moment out there, eyes flashing, over the handlebars, and challenge.

Like LeMond and Merckx, Anderson comes from a middle-class background. Not that his parents were wealthy. His mother, a ballet dancer, divorced his British father when Phil was a year old and moved back to a suburb five miles outside Melbourne. Like all Australians he can swim, but his first competitive sport was cross-country running. From there he moved onto motorbike racing – small bikes, 80 cc – until stopped by a bad crash in which he broke his right arm. He was fifteen when he saw his first bike race, a criterium at Studley Park. Amazed by the speed and danger of the cornering, he was hooked. It took a while to inquire into it, but at sixteen he was entering road races. In Australia these are all handicap races with no tactical subtlety in which those starting at scratch gang up on the weak. Phil never bothered to train, leaving his bike in the back of the car between races. A year later he found a coach. His big 56-toothed chain ring was taken away from him, his saddle was lowered, and he soon began to gain confidence. By the end of the year he had won the Victorian State 25 km time trial.

Where his club-mate Allan Peiper already knew at seventeen that he wanted a pro contract, Phil never cherished any such dream of making it to the big time. For him it was just a question of playing it day-by-day, making the state team, qualifying for the nationals, maybe winning the odd race. While still a junior, he went to New Zealand to compete in an eight-day stage race. He ended up winning it and taking the king of the mountain prize, the first Australian, let alone the first junior, ever to win it. At nineteen he went to America to prepare himself for the Commonwealth games being held in Edmonton. This speed work helped in the Commonwealth road race, as he got into the decisive three-man break and then for the first time in his life won the resulting sprint finish.

Anderson's coach had been with ACBB maestro, Mickey Wiegand, at the Noumea Six Day during which Jacques Anquetil had decided to go for an early morning swim in his tuxedo. Such events have a way of effecting a bond. When Wiegand told him there

facing page: Greg LeMond
following pages: The Irish turn out in force to watch the Nissan International Classic
climb St. Patrick's Hill in Cork

was still an ACBB place available for a foreigner, Phil accepted, thinking that racing in France might help him prepare for the forthcoming Moscow Olympics. No sooner had Phil won the second race he entered on the Riviera than Wiegand was talking of a pro contract. The more the Australian continued to win, the more the pressure increased, culminating when Anderson won the amateur version of the Grand Prix des Nations.

Anderson's misgivings must have been compounded during his first year with Peugeot. Having to serve as a domestique for riders like Duclos-Lassalle and Bossis who were not necessarily better than him, but were French, cannot have been easy. The situation is one that his Paris flat-mate of the time, Robert Millar, likewise chafed under. But as Phil said, 'At least I had Anne about to keep up my morale. Otherwise I don't think I could have made it.' Fortunately his Peugeot director De Muer was not entirely successful in curbing Anderson's over-generous attacking temperament and the Australian's first stage victory came in the Tour de l'Aude from a gutsy long-range attack made in the company of an Italian.

The Tour de l'Aude victory earned Phil his Tour de France selection. Immediately he decided he should capture the Yellow Jersey. No Australian had ever done that! Unfortunately there were a few mountains in the way. "How should I climb them?" he asked journalist John Wilcockson as they sat in his Nice hotel room on the eve of the race. 'I can climb a bit, but I've never been over anything as big as the Pyrenees.' Wilcockson suggested that he should not try to go with a true climber, but instead take the wheel of someone who climbs evenly – like Hinault. Anderson followed Wilcockson's advice to the letter, taking Hinault's wheel on the Pla d'Adet finish climb, and as a result found himself in the Yellow Jersey. That lasted, alas, only a day, but Phil had caught the bug and a year later, to prove it was no fluke, grabbed the Yellow Jersey for a second time.

One would think Peugeot might have been pleased: with the accruing publicity, the prize money and team bonuses to be shared. But they saw it for what it was, part of the ongoing war, and only one team member, Bernard Bourreau, agreed to help Phil defend his precious tunic. Nonetheless, he managed to hang onto it for another week. Almost as satisfactory was noting his improvement in the mountains. Where before he could only climb on power, in the big ring à la Hinault, now he was able to use his legs and spin at less physical cost.

That autumn Anderson did not endear himself to Peugeot when he took the unprecedented step of hiring an intermediary to negotiate his contract. What bothered him was Peugeot's assumption that they could rent out his name and image to all the other supporting companies without his seeing a penny of it. 'Everybody else lets them get away with it because they want a good-guy name for themselves,' he once explained to me. 'But what good does a name do for a cyclist in Australia? It's a short career and I have to make what money I can now.' I remember visiting his rented home in Waregem. There may have been a white Mercedes 300SL in the garage, and a bit of land in the

Mud-caked riders in Milan-San Remo climb the Turchino pass

Crash victim Ludo Peeters out of the Amstel Gold Race

Australian mountain country waiting for a house to be built on it. But there wasn't money on hand to pay for the furnishings Anne had just bought; 'I need a victory and I need it pretty quick.'

That first classic victory, with the help of Raas and Zoetemelk, came a couple of weeks later in the Amstel Gold Race and Phil was off. He was the best rider, by all accounts, in the Tour de Romandie where he took second behind team-mate Stephen Roche, and the dominating presence in a Tour of Wallonie in Belgium that he wanted to dedicate to the recently deceased head of his local fan club and which Stephen again won. 'That's cycling,' he said. "It's not every day you feel well. When you do, chances are you have to ride for someone else.' These set-backs made him all the more determined to leave Peugeot and go where he could be a team leader in his own right.

Another long breakaway ending in victory in the Tour de l'Aude seemed to point in that direction and he entered the 1983 Tour as co-favourite with the recent Swiss Tour winner Sean Kelly. Not perhaps the ideal position to be in, if you feel a bit short of your best climbing form, and I remember his striking me on the eve of the Tour in Creteil as distinctly nervous. A week earlier, because I wanted to see how one trains for the mountains, we had done a practice run of the crucial Pau-Luchon stage together with an Australian film crew and his Peugeot sub-director, Roger Legeay. It was lovely for two days to watch him, now on his arms, now in the saddle, clearly enjoying the awesome surroundings. And to watch the others, the party of cyclo-tourists in blue tunics instantaneously applauding as they recognized this embodiment of courage, or the busload of waving children higher up the same slope, who did even better–they made their bus stop so they could hop out and collect his autograph at the summit. Though the stage looked to my eyes very good for him with its long last mountain descent into Luchon, Phil himself thought that the training would have been more effective if the mountains had come early in the race, rather than after ten days in the flat.

Although Anderson arrived in Pau only a few seconds away from the Yellow Jersey, he had already dipped much too far into his reserves doing work in the heat that he had been either unwilling or unable to delegate. The rest, Simon's betrayal, then all those days of senseless waiting when Peugeot would not let him ride and he saw everything, including his prospects of a contract elsewhere, going out of the window, is history. At the same time, as so often happens, the loss of his prospects brought its own release. He slept well, his face lost its look of strain, and the next thing you knew he and Bernaudeau had almost ripped Fignon's jersey off his back and turned the Tour into a whole new event.

For the rest of the summer Anderson rode very well. His spirited presence in the Kellogg's series, lapping the field almost at will on one occasion, had much to do with its initial success as a believable event. Not part of the usual combines (the British v. the continental-based riders), he was willing to mete out his own brand of justice. When Paul Sherwen braked in front of him, causing a serious pile-up, Phil took hold of him–and Sherwen looks like the sort who can stand up for himself–and asked him whether he wanted to go out behind the bales of straw now or the next lap, 'Now,'

Phil Anderson

Sherwen replied very meekly, and out he went. Then there was the battle with Phil Thomas for the overall series lead. And battle is a term not lightly used. Knowing he had to get to the corner first to win the final sprint, Thomas began braking and swerving in front of Anderson. After crossing the line in second place Phil took him by the shoulders and slammed him almost through the pavement.

If there was one team Anderson disliked as a Peugeot rider it was the Peter Post-managed Raleigh. So it was all the stranger to hear it bruited about that he was transferring there where he would have to fit into a system and not be a unique team leader. Early in the year the Raleigh classics leader Jan Raas had announced that he was forming his own Kwantum team, taking with him the virtual core of the Raleigh team. That meant that when Post came up with Japanese sponsorship there were places open. One of them, it was generally assumed, was going to Anderson. The rumours genuinely alarmed him. 'I've had no offers from anybody,' he told me on the eve of the Worlds. 'Everybody assumes I'm going to Post, but I have never even seen him. It seems much more likely that I'll be racing in Italy.' As he talked I became aware just how difficult it was, without an agent, on your own, to change teams. Fortunately, Phil rode an excellent Worlds. He didn't win, but he was the strong man of the race, single-handedly destroying the Italians and setting the stage for LeMond's winning attack. Two weeks later, he signed with Panasonic.

One wondered how Post's new recruits, Vanderaerden, Eddy Planckaert and Anderson, were going to fit in together, but Phil for his part found Panasonic distinctly liberating. He won the Catalan Week because he had two team-mates, Peter Winnen and Steven Rooks, willing to ride him back and serve as reinforcements after being dropped on one of the last stage's hills. On Milan-San Remo he attacked in a snowstorm on the Turchino and was alone for 130 km, stopped less by the headwinds than a change to sunlight in the last hour which encouraged the peloton to doff their capes and start racing. On another long breakaway in Liège-Bastogne-Liège he was only caught in the streets of Liège, a race he would have won if he had received any help from Fignon on his wheel, or if Criquielion had not decided to throw his considerable energy into Kelly's cause. But he did win both the Frankfurt and Zurich Grands Prix and rode a very good Tour de France until stopped by a crash on a short final descent.

In 1985, benefitting from the new training methods that Moser had pioneered, he did even better, coming within a whisker of winning the Super Prestige despite a crippling lower back injury that plagued him over the last three months of the season and which kept him from racing until early June of 1986. For Phil, the important victories here were the Dauphiné (he had won an amazing stage in a blizzard the year before) and the Swiss Tour: both won, as he said, less on talent than bluff, that ability to ride up front and look the threatening part.

Bluff, of course, has always been part of Anderson's arsenal. But in the early days when he spoke of his need for it, it was always in relation to those naturally more talented, like, say, Stephen Roche. Just keeping up, staying on the same mountainside, was, one gathered, an enormous struggle. Now the issue seems more one of command, of not letting a race that one has won escape. In a very short time Phil has clearly acquired the cards to play a very mean game. For myself, I can't wait to read the book he will one day write about it. With his courage, openness, and gift for sharp, witty images it could be as good as André Leducq's *Une Fleur au guidon*.

GREG LEMOND

If anyone looks the part of the hero on his white stallion who has come roaring out of the west it is this freckle-faced American from Reno, Nevada, with the dirty blond hair and the small startlingly pale-blue eyes. As cyclists go the body is just about ideal – a slightly taller, leaner Bernard Hinault. The lung VO_2 capacity is far larger than that of any other American cyclist. Junior World Road Champion in 1979, World Champion and Super Prestige best rider of the year in 1983, winner of the 1986 Tour de France, Greg LeMond is far and away America's greatest ever road racer as well as a thoroughly likable young man.

But for all his achievements and obvious class LeMond has still a great deal to prove before he is accepted as anything like Hinault's successor. The Tour de France victory was not only his first big victory of 1986. It was his first substantial victory, the Coors Classic and a time trial stage of the previous year's Tour de France aside, since the 1983 Worlds. In between Greg took a great many second places; enough to have earned him in the French press the sobriquet of the 'American Poulidor' (the 'eternal second' of the 1960s). But in cycling only one place counts – first – and LeMond has not won enough as yet to stamp the sport with his personality.

There are a number of reasons given for LeMond not winning more often. For Laurent Fignon, who rode on the same Renault team as LeMond until 1985, the American 'isn't a leader. He doesn't take the risks to win and thus he can't win. He's an excellent second, but not a winner.' Harsh words, but from someone who rode often enough as LeMond's domestique, they do carry a certain weight. Fignon's remarks about LeMond not being a leader are echoed by the American's best friend in the pack, Phil Anderson. Speaking from his own two-time experience of having held the Yellow Jersey in the Tour de France, he says: 'Taking the Yellow Jersey means a lot more than just the jersey. You have to defend it and assume the weight of the course. Hinault does that. He controls the racing macho-like: staying at the front, pushing a huge gear, daring others to come around him, growling. You have to earn the respect of the other riders and it's all a bluff, but like I found out in the Dauphiné and Tour de Suisse (both of which the Australian won in 1985) you have to play the game if you want to be a leader. I don't think Greg has learned all this yet.'

Such explanations, fascinating as they are, inevitably say more about Fignon and Anderson than about LeMond. LeMond's problem goes a good deal deeper than a mere question of leadership, of a tendency to panic when the chips are down. Talk to Fignon or Anderson and they are wholly in front of you, inventing themselves afresh. Talk to LeMond and you can't believe that what he is telling you he hasn't said a great many times already. In the American cycling press he is often accused of contradicting himself, imparting one bit of gospel one moment, the opposite advice a few months later. Fine, the more courage to him; at least he is willing to speak out with an honesty that is refreshing in comparison to a Hinault or Moser. The trouble is rather that his views don't really belong to him, they are so much received wisdom, his father's, his coach's. Perhaps that's why his conversation so frequently includes the word 'frankly', as if he were making a great effort to bring himself back, to seem to be there in front of you.

This problem isn't merely LeMond's; it is that of a great many American sports stars: desperately eager, like LeMond, to talk to you – a fellow American! – at one moment; at the next distractedly squirming, eyes fixed on that main chance in the media cap about to walk by. The problem is compounded when you represent a minority sport. You win the world championships and, instead of a whole nation jumping up and down in glee, you get barely a two-inch mention. Before winning the Tour de France LeMond was much better known for his colour commentary on the Los Angeles Olympic road race than for anything he himself had achieved on the road.

When your eye is focussed elsewhere, it is hard to concentrate on the matter at hand, whether it's winning a race or truly explaining yourself to a reporter. Instead you are confecting this image, this national hero on the white horse. And because of the nature of American television, never able to let events speak for themselves, always trivializing, the image you are selling is bound to be a much shrunken version of yourself; rating yourself on how much in salary you are able to command, rather than what you have accomplished which, you feel, no one will understand. Worse still, all that you are marketing through the image – the sunglasses on your head, the shoes that don't really fit your heat-swollen feet – tends to overshadow the actual business of riding. That's why LeMond is so often bored in a race. How can getting in the right break compare for excitement with all those deals his fellow riders report him talking about, his property investments, his lawsuits, the salesman or journalist he will see after the race. For LeMond, one feels, it is the rare event that gets ridden for itself. The Worlds, yes, that's practically his own name, LeMond in English, and time after time he has gotten himself up for it. And the Tour de France, that is big enough, worth the year out of his life that his team-mate Hampsten has said each edition is costing him. As for the rest . . . it starts to be like Jonathan Boyer riding Bordeaux-Paris without sufficient preparation because Bordeaux is one town your countrymen have heard of – and because one underestimates the opposition. It's all, alas, so American.

Talking to LeMond it's hard to know what he feels about the sport. Cycling may still mean a great deal to him – if not so much as golf – but his involvement has become hidden behind all those other things that are expected of an American sportsman: to be competitive, aggressive, a money-winner. Like John McEnroe, LeMond gives less and less the impression of enjoying what he is doing – one reason why he keeps getting into scraps with television cameramen. And that notion of always being the outsider, of life conducted on xenophobic lines ('I'd like to see a Frenchman go to America at nineteen, get a pro baseball contract and do what I've done') develops into paranoia: 'You always have to go through dope control . . . This sport is so nationalistic. I just wonder how far the organizers will go to have Hinault win.'; 'If they are going to knock me into a ditch . . .' 'I'll quit the race.' As *Sports Illustrated* in their article on the 1986 Worlds pointed out, he has now become a 'world-class whiner'.

LeMond was fourteen and a crack acrobatic skier when a race, the Northern

California/Nevada district championships, happened to come by his house. That looked like fun and he took it up as a way of maintaining form for skiing. Along came the great California drought of 1976-77. Obliged to ride right through the winter, he found himself hooked. He was also fortunate in being able to share his discovery of the sport with his father, a highly successful real estate operator, who quickly became a top veteran-class rider.

In two years LeMond progressed to the point where he was national junior champion. By the time he won the Junior Worlds and two other medals at Buenos Aires, he was already better than any senior US rider. While still a junior, he took fourth in the Colorado Red Zinger, and might have won on the last day but for a crash. He served notice he was ready to become a professional next spring when, still eighteen, he won the pro-amateur Circuit de la Sarthe. But it was the manner in which he refused to allow the Russians to intimidate him in a stage race of that same spring, the Ruban Granitier Breton, that caught the eye of Cyrille Guimard. Guimard had signed Bernard Hinault for Gitane-Renault as a nineteen-year-old and brought him along in a carefully designed three-year programme. There was no reason why, he thought, the very similar talent of this young American could not be developed in the same scientific way.

LeMond liked the Reno-Sacramento area he was from and did not relish being thrust into a foreign culture. And his family looked askance at what they saw as the snake-pit of European cycling, the physical abuse, the drugs, and all the rest of it. But Greg did not have many alternatives. College held no particular attraction and there was not as yet any developed professional circuit in America. Like it or not, Europe was where one had to go if one wanted to reach one's true potential. As LeMond said, 'You have to get used to suffering day after day, month after month–to be on the verge of cracking, but not crack. That's a lesson I learned in Europe when I was nineteen years old.' Given such a choice, there seemed no better coach to work with than the thirty-one-year-old Guimard.

Guimard, for his part, bent over backward to accommodate the LeMonds. He found Greg a house near him in Anjou. To help make the transition and language problems easier he hired as a fellow team-rider for Hinault LeMond's countryman Jonathan Boyer, who speaks excellent French. And, along with LeMond's reputed $50,000 salary, the largest ever offered a new pro, he agreed to a programme that would allow Greg to keep returning every few months to the United States.

Not all of this worked out quite as planned. Boyer is a much more closed, secretive person than LeMond and the two did not get on. And Greg and his vivacious, equally young, wife Kathy felt isolated in the French countryside. After two years she had made only one friend. With the encouragement of the Andersons they moved to Kortrijk, Belgium, where, among other things, they could tune into British television. For a year or so thereafter the French cycling mags, who obviously felt snubbed, featured pictures of the young people standing alongside their wallscreen TV with its remote control focussing and video recorder.

For a first-year pro LeMond did pretty well, taking a third in the Dauphiné Libéré behind Hinault, and outsmarting a posse of bullying Russians to win the Coors Classic. There must have been a great deal to be learned from working as a domestique for

Hinault, who was impressed enough to dub the young American his heir apparent. If Hinault himself was hard to get close to, there was a good *esprit de corps* among the young Renault hot-shots, Marc Madiot, Fignon, Pascal Jules, Vincent Barteau, from all reports very good company.

LeMond was not well prepared to ride the 1982 Worlds; nonetheless he came in second. He followed it up by winning the apprentice Tour de France, the Tour de l'Avenir, by some ten minutes, impressing everyone with the fluency of his climbing. On the strength of that it was not surprising to see Greg installed as the Renault early season leader, while Hinault prepared in his own slow fashion for the Vuelta, his first appointment of the year.

LeMond did not arrive in shape for the spring campaign. 'I didn't ride enough miles this winter,' he told me when I saw him after the Flèche Wallonne. When I repeated that later the same evening to Anderson, Phil said, 'He rode a helluva lot more miles than I did. Then, everybody is different.' As far as I could see LeMond had his own timetable, the Dauphiné Libéré and the Swiss Tour for 1983, the Tour de France for 1984; the rest did not really count. LeMond himself disagreed, 'I should be winning more. That's what I am being paid for. But I guess I have time.' One could see LeMond's point. If you are being paid a big salary, you are expected to produce. On the other hand, it might be argued that LeMond's salary had more to do with his potential and with his being the American the industry needed than with the immediate present. When your real career lies ahead of you, the last thing anyone wants is for you to burn yourself out.

The Spanish Vuelta into which LeMond was drafted a week later as a last-minute replacement was particularly gruesome. For the first time he began to wonder what he was doing trying to make a living on a bike. The experience may explain why, after winning the Dauphiné and looming fourth to Kelly in the Swiss Tour, he stuck to his time-table and refused to lead the Renault team in Hinault's absence. 'The Tour de France is not something you throw yourself into at the last minute,' he said. On the other side, one may well wonder why not? He and Guimard had ample warning, he was in form; it was just that he had this script –'I am going to win the Tour the first time I ride it like Bernard and Eddy and the other greats'– that had to be adhered to. When your possibilities are that circumscribed, you don't take the necessary chances.

The rest is history, or Fignon, who emerged from almost nowhere to take the Tour, while Greg watched it on TV from his California home. But Fignon's example seems to have inspired LeMond. He trained hard for the Worlds with Phil Anderson and won it impressively. Though time-trialling is not something he enjoys (other than in the context of a stage race), he trained for the Grand Prix des Nations equally hard and was rewarded with forty-five second-place points. On the basis of this late charge he was right on course for the Super Prestige Pernod award. All he had to do was not let Kelly beat him by more than two places in Tour of Lombardy. Not the easiest of tasks as Greg found himself dropped on the first hill and again in difficulties on the San Fermo climb at the very end. But he recovered well enough to be on Kelly's wheel as the final sprint manoeuvring began. Kelly won for his first major classic victory, but a tyre's width behind the line was LeMond (barely ahead of four others). If that isn't class, I don't know what is.

Hinault's rupture with Guimard, which led to the forming of his own La Vie Claire team, may have eased LeMond's mind about staying with Renault. Despite having to share the team leadership with Fignon, he signed a several-year contract for $180,000 plus benefits (making him higher paid than Fignon even though the Frenchman had won the Tour). This put the struggle for house supremacy down to one race, the 1984 Tour de France. Would the American win it on his debut, or would Fignon, or – rather more likely – Hinault? While Fignon took on the added risk of the Giro-Tour back-to-back double, LeMond put his whole season into readying himself for the Tour. But something went wrong, Greg caught bronchitis, and he was never really in the race, even though he finished third. When the post-race smoke had cleared LeMond found himself the number two rider at Renault.

Greg LeMond wearing the Rainbow Jersey in the 1983 Tour of Lombardy

Even before the start of the 1984 Tour Hinault had realised he would have to strengthen his La Vie Claire team if he was to enter the history books with a record-tying fifth Tour de France win. Accordingly he went to Fignon, who told him he was tied to Renault for at least another year. After the Tour he approached Stephen Roche, but Roche too was still in the middle of a contract with La Redoute. So, Hinault and the La Vie Claire owner, Bernard Tapie, decided to go after LeMond, offering the American a three-year million dollar contract. Guimard did not like having his investment in LeMond pilfered, least of all by Hinault; but Renault was becoming increasingly strapped for funds – they would abandon the sport a year later – and one can see that letting LeMond and his big salary go could help clarify things for Fignon, Madiot and company.

Questioned as to why he was paying LeMond a million dollars, Tapie replied that if LeMond were French he would be worth one less zero. Looked at as a means of penetrating a market, LeMond's salary was cheap compared to what one of his companies, Look Ski and Cycle, was already paying out in American advertising.

LeMond was not Tapie's only acquisition. Before going after LeMond he had already signed the 1983 Tour de France Yellow Jersey-wearer, Dane Kim Andersen. Now to ease LeMond's isolation he signed the Olympic runner-up, Steve Bauer. And he followed this up by adding three more Americans for 1986; climber Andy Hampsten, who would win the Tour of Switzerland; Thurlow Rogers; and a rider from whom we are bound to hear in future years, Roy Knickman.

With LeMond at his side and no Fignon to compete against, Hinault duly won the 1985 Tour de France. Not surprisingly, LeMond expected him to return the favour in 1986; a deal is a deal. Asked about it before the race, Hinault hemmed and hawed; 'In principle, I am supposed to support LeMond in return for his help last year. But who knows what I'll feel like when I'm in the middle of the race.' The race is history – or rather, soap opera. And nothing summed it up better than to peek into the La Vie Claire restaurant at L'Alpe d'Huez and see Hinault with his French team-mates at one table, LeMond, Bauer, and Hampsten at another, and the two Swiss, Winterburg and Ruttimann, observing their national tradition of strict impartiality at a third, but rather nearer the North Americans. LeMond claims to have had few allies within the pack. That may be, but at crucial moments, when his own hands were tied, there were Millar and Anderson's Panasonics more than willing to save his bacon for him.

LeMond is still very young and there is a great deal he can do to change our perceptions of him and of his sport. One may not like his business-oriented approach; but for the sport as a whole it may not be such a bad thing. Riders may not as yet be where tennis players are; but thanks to the new money (much of it dollars) that Tapie and LeMond have brought into the sport, their situation has markedly improved of late. If LeMond's troubles with Hinault persuade him to mount an English-speaking team, that too could be highly positive. One only hopes that, as the sport takes on a more and more global dimension, the season as we know it with its beautiful inner coherence does not get swept away.

PART THREE · THE SEASON

Phil Anderson, Michel Pollentier and Luc Colijn battle through chilling rain in the 1983
Tour of Flanders

IN MOST PROFESSIONAL SPORTS the athletes hop about from venue to venue, continent to continent, seemingly at random. While we can admire the ease with which they pass through the time-zones, it is hard to view their sports as anything other than a never-ending, year-round treasure hunt. Not that this does not carry its special fascination; but in such a sporting world cycling stands out as one of the few sports that has a real season. This is because cycling is an outdoor sport *par excellence.* At every moment the riders are at the mercy of the elements, whether it's the Riviera in February or the mountains of the Tour de France in July. Like the gods of old, a rider is popularly identified with the terrain he has conquered: when we recall Eddy Merckx's arch-rival Roger De Vlaeminck it is the mud and cobbles of Paris-Roubaix that we see rather than the arms-in-the-air sprint finisher.

Just as there is within every stage race a day's event and an overall classification, so one event traditionally prepares another and is viewed in the context of the entire season. A rider competes in the mid-March Paris-Nice or the cross-Italy Tirreno-Adriatico to get in shape for the spring-opening 'Primavera', Milan-San Remo, while the *classicissima,* as the Italians fondly call it, leads into the series of northern cobblestone classics, Paris-Roubaix and the Tour of Flanders. From Flanders move a few miles into French-speaking Belgium and we have the two hill classics, the Flèche Wallonne and Liège-Bastogne-Liège. Once introduced, this hill theme continues into the stage races that will now preoccupy us; climbing races like the Swiss Tour de Romandie and the Dauphiné Libéré in French Savoy; national Tours like the Spanish Vuelta and the Italian Giro, all of which climax in the Tour de France. Again, the world championships road race in the first week of September reintroduces the theme of the classics, running from Paris-Brussels to the Grand Prix d'Automne and the beautiful season-ending Tour of Lombardy.

Such progressions stood out, no doubt, more clearly fifty years ago when the racing calendar was not the increasingly congested thing it has become. If the season ended with the Tour of Lombardy around Lake Como, then, observing the unities, it made sense for it to open a few miles away with Milan-San Remo. And the long 292 km format of Milan-San Remo on the primitive roads of that time, out of the winter leaflessness of the Po, over the Turchino Pass, and down to the Riviera, had all the trappings of high drama. If, despite the often execrable weather, vast numbers lined the roadway, it was because they saw the riders as their champions, venturing forth like the fisher-kings of old to fetch the sun out of its winter cave.

From a competitive standpoint 292 km might seem a lot to ask of a rider's muscles for his first outing of the year. It was to give the men of the north a means of preparing Milan-San Remo and the April round of Belgian classics that Jean Leuillot originally organized Paris-Nice. It fitted in all the better in that it too could be billed as a race to the sun – a Riviera made all the more rewarding by the hazards of mountains and inclement weather so often encountered on the way.

Paris-Nice succeeded beyond anything Leuillot envisaged. But this very success meant that the riders now had another and much longer race to prepare. Gone are the days when, with a mere 1700 km in his legs, a rider could hop on a bike and, like Jacques Anquetil, count on winning. Now that Paris-Nice has become an authentic test in its own right, a rider needs five times as much, something the whole February programme exists to prepare. In Spain it takes place in Andalusia; in Italy, in Sicily before moving to Sardinia; and in France it starts earliest of all with a bracing week in Bessèges in the Cevennes foothills before transferring across the Rhône for another three and a half weeks in the Riviera back country between Grasse and Draguignan.

RIVIERA TRAINING CAMPS

Early February might seem an odd time of year to launch a cycling season. But after a January broken up by medical check-ups, visits to the team factories, an official team presentation, a week in the snow to 'oxygenate', and, on the more positive side, maybe some Sunday cyclo-cross, anything that will let a rider settle down and build up the necessary miles in his legs is bound to be appreciated.

By the time the riders convene in the South of France, or wherever their training camps lie, most of the preliminary work of *souplesse,* of lengthening and stretching the heart muscle, has presumably been accomplished. From the beginning of December onwards, to the extent that the roads permit, the riders will have been cycling two or three hours a day, always on the small chain ring, and hopefully in the wind. They will also have put in a considerable number of hours jogging, playing tennis or squash, and doing weight work in a gym to strengthen the lower back and arms; not trying for more muscle, but muscle tone.

The amount of mileage needed in the legs to be fit varies from one rider to another. To guide them and help them peak for their major objectives all riders keep a diary in which they note mileage, what they have been eating, course conditions, and the like. Once this initial stamina has been built up work can begin on resistance, i.e. strengthening the walls of the heart. Since this involves some sharpening of speeds, certain riders like to take part in one or two Six Day events before heading south, a practice that explains much of the Kwantum and Panasonic riders' domination of the initial Bessèges week. But riding these all-night races on an indoor track with all that cigarette smoke filling the lungs may not be so good for general health.

For this work most observers feel that a training camp in the Riviera foothills, within an hour and a half's drive of the fabled 'azure' coast and the every-other-day races, but at nearly 500 m high enough to stimulate the heart, is an obvious desideratum. The first half of February is apt to be the coldest time of the continental year and most riders would prefer to be on the Riviera itself with the possibility of doing a bit of sailing, or taking in a nightspot, rather than in these bleak foothills. But the isolation is a central feature of these oversized, package tour hotels in which they are stuck, for riders do not normally live together as a squad; as soon as an event or the series for which they have been summoned is over they head home, and they stay there, bearing their own expenses, until once again summoned to a race. For this reason a training camp assumes a real importance, because it is the one time when they are all together. If a team spirit is to be forged, it must be done here.

This emphasis on camaraderie carries over into the daily 180 km training sessions, which may strike an outside observer as all too casual: a double line pedalling briskly along with as much horseplay as can be improvised. The routine usually consists of 90 minutes in the late morning (if there is no photographic session scheduled), followed after lunch by another couple of hours climbing in the stark *garrigue* hill country for those not involved in a race. Riders who want to get more 'spin' into their legs may want to tack on another twenty minutes on rollers (rather like working out with a kickboard in a swimming pool). It is not uncommon to see riders pedalling back to their hotels after a coastal race.

Also life in a training camp, it being France, revolves less around the road than the table, and here discipline is very much in evidence. The riders may cross a room to shake a visitor's hand before a meal, but once the courses start, the pâtés and fish and meat and salad and cheese, followed by any number of desserts, there is no breaking in on them. Except for the absence of sauces, the food does not greatly differ from what one would eat if one had anything like their 5000 calorie capacity: coffee and croissants for breakfast (no fresh fruit, no health food cereal until recently); wine at lunch and dinner. Since the hotels are often owned by cooks, the fare may stray to the gourmet side. But the emphasis is less on eating healthily than staying within the culture. If after dinner and the usual team meeting a rider feels like visiting his wife or girl-friend at her secret lodgings in the next village, that's his affair.

Just as this grape and olive-growing country with its tiled, flat-roofed farms is Roman, or Roman-influenced, so these fortified hill towns – Seillans, Fayence, Montauroux – have a Tuscan air. It is here, of course, that bicycling with its myth of the sun fits in; nor is it any accident that many of these training races, including the season-opening Tour du Haut Var, are sponsored by people in the local construction industry.

PRE-SEASON RACES

It is current fashion to play down these every-other-day pre-season races. Judged by the standards of the only truly serious race among them, the Tour du Haut Var, they leave a lot to be desired in the virtual absence of a public and in their attention to riders' safety. At this time of year the municipalities involved are not inclined to spend what they should on policing to ensure that the roads are properly sealed off. Instead they shunt the riders on to comparatively unused roads and just hope. To descend at 100 kmph on a supposedly closed circuit and see cars coming right up at you can be rather unnerving. When it happens twice you may feel justified in calling it a day.

The danger is compounded by the presence of a large number of newcomers up from the amateur ranks who are not as yet accustomed to the demands of cornering, descending, and sprinting in a tight pack, let alone the very style of professional racing. In the circumstances one can see why riders with mid-season objectives might prefer to stay at home and train on their own. But training on your own lacks the competitive sharpness that racing brings about. And with no opportunity to check yourself out you can leave it all until too late. It was interesting to note that one late arrival of these last years, Phil Anderson, was at Bessèges in 1985 for the first time in his career. He went on to have a season that would have won him the best rider of the year award except for a late-season back injury and a certain Sean Kelly.

Races, like the Riviera-opening Grand Prix d'Antibes, are spirited affairs. 'Wow!' I remember Allan Peiper remarking afterwards, 'it's like going from kindergarten to college.' At this time of the year bodies are still fresh and eager to prove something – to themselves if not one another – while the professional ranks are swollen by newcomers like Peiper hoping to spring a surprise while they still can. And in a profession where morale, willpower, counts for so much, each team wants to get off to the best possible start. Courses like the Monaco Grand Prix with its climbs onto the corniches and descents back into the town (using the same tunnel as the celebrated car race), or the decisive Mont Faron climb with its 16 per cent gradient in the Mediterranean Tour, are more than capable of inspiring a lively race.

The Tour du Haut Var, located in the training camp country between Draguignan and Seillans, marks the formal adieu to this pre-season phase, if not to the region (Paris-Nice uses some of the same roads). The climbs for which the classic is known are hardly severe, except for the last over Mons. But with half a dozen on the menu they are enough to disrupt a pack and ensure a lively battle. Such winners in recent years as Zoetemelk, Millar and Pascal Simon suggest the standard of the confrontation.

HET VOLK

After a month's racing around the Mediterranean the good folk in Belgium grow understandably anxious. Where are our riders? Are they ever coming back? It is partly to reassure this most fanatic of cycling publics that *Het Volk*, a tabloid-format Ghent daily, has instituted on the eve of Paris-Nice its winter classic, the first of those counting for the Pernod Super Prestige best rider-of-the-year award.

By Tour of Flanders standards (which borrows to more effect much of the same Flemish Ardennes terrain), the 240 km loop may seem relatively undemanding. From a sporting point of view the first 120 km ridden on wide flat roads offer very little other than the odd inevitable crash caused by the fifteen to twenty team congestion and the slowness of the pace. But the pace starts to heat up as the race approaches the Old Kwaremont hill where the wide road suddenly narrows to a 4 m wide cobbled lane. Because of the likelihood of a crash, to have a chance in the race you have to be in the first twenty over the hill, and the competition for these prime places is, to say the least, very spirited. By the top of the Kwaremont a lead peloton of about fifty riders should be left, followed at 15-second intervals by smaller chasing groups.

Normally such intervals would be closed in a few miles. But the rapid succession with which the Eikenberg, Volkegemberg, Leberg and Berendries come, and the way the mostly cobbled lanes turn through the brick villages, around grassy hillocks and over the odd rail crossing, is from a chasing point of view discouraging, as you have nothing to measure yourself by. And the pace does not decrease. Only the strongest, the best prepared, survive.

The climax of this section of hills is the infamous Geraardesbergen, better known by its French name, the Mur de Grammont. The Grammont is relatively short, 180 metres at most. But the shortness means you don't have time to gear down and when the

The Mur de Grammont in the rain proves too much for Eric Vanderaerden, lying on the ground

In 1986 the Het Volk did not start at all!

De Wolf and Raas take flight from the pursuing field in the 1983 Het Volk

20 per cent wall finally hits – the steepest in all cycling – you may find yourself like Eric Vanderaerden, the leader up it in the 1985 race (the 1986 was cancelled because a series of snowstorms had made the roads impassable), losing momentum to such an extent that he spun out of control and crashed.

Such crashes are made all the more serious because halfway through the next village of Zottegem, at a Honda garage, the race turns suddenly left at the Paddestraat (Toad Street). This cobbled street is not a hill. But 6 km of huge, broken stones do not make for easy riding and in bad weather they can be well-nigh impassable. It is here that the decisive break of the race often occurs, even though the town of Ghent is still some 40 km distant and the roads wide and well-paved.

Races like the Het Volk are very hard to see, much less photograph, because the cobbles keep one from getting near to the riders. But Watson's shot of Alfons De Wolf with Jan Raas struggling on his wheel (taken as they are emerging from the Volkegemberg) *is* the 1983 Het Volk, even though they are still some 40 km from the Ghent finish. The picture may look as if it has been taken from a motorcycle, but it is actually taken from a curve at a bank of the road where he happened to be standing (his motorcycle had crashed out for good only moments earlier). This is a race that De Wolf, starting out for Bianchi and intent on proving himself after a disastrous previous season, had to win. Such was the general knowledge of these imperatives that Raas was to be accused afterwards of selling out to De Wolf, a far inferior sprinter. But one look at Raas's face and one can see how he is doing everything he can just to hold De Wolf's wheel.

That the two, within a few miles, were able to build a lead of several minutes against a determined pack shows a remarkable superiority. Oddly, De Wolf timed the Het Volk just right; the last explosion of a firefly-like career.

PARIS-NICE

As French stage races go, Paris-Nice may not compare with the Alpine rigours of the June Dauphiné. But the 'race to the sun' is France's second longest event and enjoys a far greater hold on the sporting public. This may have something to do with its coming at a time when the sports pages are relatively uncluttered, and with the evocative pictures sent back of grim-faced riders pedalling through the appalling weather so often encountered during March.

How important this one event is can be seen in what victory here in 1982 meant to Sean Kelly. Not only was his career transformed – before that he was a sprinter and nothing more – but his whole personality flowered. He talked more volubly, rode differently, and at the end of the year even got married. And he has made sure that he has won the event every year since.

Monde Six, the organization that promotes Paris-Nice, the Trophée des Grimpeurs and the autumnal Étoile des Espoirs, puts the accent on the sporting aspect of cycling. It is not totally oriented towards commercial profit like many other big race organizers.

Sean Kelly wins the Col d'Eze time trial and the Paris-Nice race overall in 1983

Often enough the 'race to the sun' has to make its way through the snow first...

That policy dates back to the founder of Paris-Nice, Jean Leuillot, a one-time poet and artist who was one of France's foremost cycling journalists until his death in 1982. His vision of the event and his romantic image of bicycle racing are alive today because of his two daughters, Josette and Jacqueline, who run Monde Six with the help of publicist André Hardy. After a number of years in Paris's Latin Quarter they now work out of an anonymous white house in Issy-les-Moulineaux, an inner Paris suburb not far from the Eiffel Tower. When you step into their offices, you realize that a different spirit reigns over this race compared with the slick, corporate commercialism of the Tour de France. At Monde Six you don't need formal appointments; they will sit you down with coffee and a liqueur and perhaps give you a talk on race organization.

On the Tour de France the reporter may receive a sacred green press badge, but the hospitality virtually stops there and even seeing a pair of pedalling legs requires luck. On Paris-Nice, however, the welcome mat is laid out for every race follower, many of whom take a week's vacation from their normal employment to do a volunteer job. The organization pays for meals, gas and lodgings; in return the volunteer is expected to work a 12 to 15-hour day. In France, unlike such countries as Belgium, the road police have to be paid by the race organizers. Since some teams too have to be paid, Monde Six has to do everything it can to cut corners to be able to offer the riders this race. Many of the official drivers are former racers or cycling club presidents. The 1937 Tour de France winner, Roger Lapébie, is a frequent driver. For the journalist, covering the race is a simple task in comparison with the Tour de France. The organizers provide every car with a race information radio receiver, and they place few restrictions on watching the action from close quarters.

In a male-dominated sport what makes Paris-Nice so different are the Leuillot sisters. Intelligent, open, and hard-working, they command loyalty. Adding to the general conviviality is the presence of race director Jacques Anquetil. As a rider, Anquetil had the reputation of being a cold, calculating fish, keeping anything from happening on the stages and winning on sheer power through his prowess as a time triallist. But he was also known for the lightness with which he viewed training and that champagne side of his character remains, along with his substantial intelligence. Unlike so many who have crossed into management, Anquetil is firmly on the riders' side, knowing that they make the race and must be supported.

To have a race that captures the public imagination year after year you must have a competitive course. If Paris-Nice has succeeded in this respect it is because the tension rarely lapses. Stage by stage the interest builds to reach a dramatic finale in the spectacular Col d'Eze time trial over the Bay of Nice. Credit here should go to André Hardy. It is he who sets out for a month every autumn to drive the prospective routes of Paris-Nice. With him are a tape recorder and log book into which goes all the information he has dictated each day: safety precautions, a street narrowing or island in the road, crossings where police will have to be posted, railway gates to be checked

Sean Kelly acknowledges the crowd's salute for his record-breaking fifth successive win in Paris-Nice. Race director Jacques Anquetil – who held the previous record – stands next to him.

against timetables. For a mountain stage there usually has to be both the announced route and an alternative in case of snow.

Although some of the battle points are by now traditional, Paris-Nice still manages to include a considerable amount of new terrain every year. To do this and do it properly requires hard work, but it is what Hardy believes keeps Paris-Nice an adventure for one and all. A good race is Hardy's reward, but there is additional gratification when unsolicited donations flow in from municipalities through which the race has passed.

MILAN-SAN REMO

After Paris-Nice and Tirreno-Adriatico, Milan-San Remo represents the first gathering of the cycling clans. And it is a moving sight to see, on the eve of this 292 km race, 300 riders beneath the Sforzesco castle's sumptuous arcades going through the torchlit signing ceremonies. At that moment one can very well feel what a tradition is, and has been.

This same excitement can be felt among the one and a half million people lining the route of this race to the sea; more than for any race I have ever seen, and a testimony to the passion this sport holds for the Italian imagination. All the more remarkable in that, instead of standing in the inclement weather, they could be at home in front of their

1983: the Poggio climb near the end of Milan-San Remo. As soon as the leading rider, Ruperez, is caught, Giuseppe Saronni (Number 57) will make his winning counter-attack.

Saronni crosses the finishing line to win the 1983 Milan-San Remo. Races like this are only made possible by massive commercial sponsorship.

television sets. They are there to salute something, and if that something is more these days a procession than a race, that does not mean that these begrimed figures from the far corners of the cycling world don't deserve this respect. They are doing their best, it's just that the roads are a far cry from the dusty pitted affairs they were in 1906.

The first segment of the race across the Lombardy plain to the foot of the Turchino pass can be dangerous because of the vast numbers jammed elbow to elbow. But it is apt to be uneventful barring the sort of tail wind that helped two first-year French professionals, Marc Gomez and Alain Bondue, stay away on a record 272 km jaunt in 1982.

As the race enters the Turchino the riders' faces start reflecting the mud that is being ground up from one wheel after another into them. At the same time the faces of those watching take on a look, a desperation, that very much fit this passage of cycling history: ragged sweaters, people who know that this is the first and last time anybody is likely to drive by them for another year. But the road up is a wide and gentle ramp, nowhere near as steep as the descent, and near the top it is cut by a considerable tunnel as it would not have been when the legend of the race was being forged. Since this is the only obstacle of any consequence in the whole race riders have been known to gamble here, even though one is still a good four hours from San Remo, and Phil Anderson came very close to pulling it off in 1984.

In the old days the series of headlands offered the decisive battlepoints. But the roads and the art of defence have improved to a point where they no longer offer a viable ramp. Rather than have the peloton burst several hundred strong on to San Remo's Via Roma the organizers have instituted a pair of last-minute climbs, that of the Cipressa followed by the Poggio. Neither is much of a hill, but the descents of the Cipressa and Poggio are so dangerous (it is here that Raas ended his career) that the first over the top has a good chance of finishing alone, a tactic seven-time winner Eddy Merckx employed to good effect on a number of occasions.

Italians like sprint finishes and the San Remo finish with its packed spectators on platforms engulfing the Via Roma offers a wall of sound that for sheer volume must compare favourably with anything the Peninsula has to offer.

Milan-San Remo is not, as 1986 winner Sean Kelly remarked, 'a very good race to ride. But it is a very good race to win.' After such a long, begrimed and, it must be said, boring build-up, to see this ancient event come alive in those last few crowded feet, whether of the Cipressa summit or the Poggio, and know you are strong enough to have outfoxed everyone, must be quite satisfactory.

COBBLESTONE CLASSICS

After these races to the sun of Paris-Nice and Milan-San Remo the riders bring this sun north with them to Belgium for a two-week round of early April classics. This comprises a first, mainly Flemish, segment devoted essentially to cobbles and consisting of the Tour of Flanders, Ghent-Wevelgem, and Paris-Roubaix, followed by a rather hillier week in the French-speaking Ardennes that will culminate in the Flèche Wallonne and Liège-Bastogne-Liège. Except for Ghent-Wevelgem, they are all rugged, superbly contested races and one can see why, for many riders, they represent the high point of the season.

Judged by the crowds of Milan-San Remo, it is the Italians and not the Belgians who care most passionately about the sport. But bike-racing is rooted in the Belgian, and particularly Flemish, character at a depth that no Italian sport can begin to approach. Watching a great race in Flanders, one can feel oneself entering the soul of a people; a rather dour soul at that, it must be added. But then it's not given to everyone to have to make a living out of the wind and mud and ceaseless rain of the North Sea coast, in a congested land that has been the virtual cockpit of Northern Europe for the past 500 years. For most of us riding a bike is an essentially good-weather, summer occupation. When we go out, it is asphalt we want rather than machine-and-spine-rattling cobbles. But to the Flemish imagination, cobbles are to a surfaced road what poetry is to prose. One may not like the bump-bump-bump of the slowing down, but one can perhaps see the singular concentration it takes to keep to the crested line at the top of all this broken matter.

Hennie Kuiper of Holland jubilant at winning the 1985 Milan-San Remo

Not the First World War, but 'a line of poplars reflected in the cobbled water': the Tour of Flanders 1983

How much can he suffer, you ask as you ride along behind a Van de Velde during a later part of Paris-Roubaix, watching the flesh of his thin upper arms shaking as if it were being pounded by a drill. Just as cobbles are a Flemish-Picard specialty – 'Belgian bricks' we call them in America – so it is the suffering aspect of bike racing with which the Belgian most readily identifies.

TOUR OF FLANDERS

As a spectator one may not quite agree with Jan Raas that the Tour of Flanders is the greatest of the single-day events. But a harder, more quintessentially Flemish race does not bear imagining. Its 272 km is only 20 km short of Milan-San Remo, and what it lacks in length it more than makes up for in cobbled climbs: thirteen on the 1982 menu, a

Under the eyes of Italian television, Canada's Steve Bauer leads a Milan-San Remo breakaway up the climb of the Cipressa

Two great cobble kings: Roger De Vlaeminck and Jan Raas in the 1979 Tour of Flanders

The famous Koppenberg hill – Bernard Hinault's 'cochonnerie'

marked hardening over the four scheduled as recently as 1972. These *monts* may look like pimples on a contoured map, but a wall like the Grammont or the Koppenberg is still a 1 in 4 climb. And the frequency with which they pop up in the last half of the race is such that a rider never has time to recover before the next uphill sprint (with its possibilities of puncture, chasing, and the rest of it) is upon him.

In Antwerp on the eve of the 1983 race it was interesting to note on the hotel television set not a mention of favourites and betting odds, all that disfigured the local tabloids. Instead we were favoured with pictures of the roads themselves: a line of poplars reflected in the cobbled water; the honoured farmer through whose miry gateway the race suddenly veered with a right as lethal as a Joe Louis punch. A race, it seemed, in which the riders were mere stars, glints between the cobbles.

Just as pebbles lose all their colour when taken away from the seashore, so cobbles to be at their most effective require a covering of water. In a country where it can rain 359 days in a year this shouldn't be hard to come by. Nonetheless we hadn't had a true, wet Tour of Flanders in something like seven years and it was with the anticipation of a herd of camels emerging from the desert that we found ourselves on Easter morning trudging from the station to the Saint Niklaas town square, the largest in Belgium, where the race would start before the old town hall. For on Good Friday a fine rain had come down to slick the cobblestones and bury fragments of roadway, and it had been followed by another good drenching in the early hours of this very morning – enough to produce a snail-like contentment as we assembled in the great square. In Flanders weather conditions can be as mercurial as in England, a fact underlined in the race director's sombre greeting: 'I welcome one and all of you, but you should know, alas, that the climatic conditions are not those of a true Tour of Flanders.'

The lack of rain hardly discouraged the riders; during the first half hour a series of attacks kept the tempo well over 50 kmph. But forewarned is forearmed and the Raleighs were determined not to let anything like team rider René Martens' 1982 winnning breakaway be repeated. Nonetheless, as we headed westwards towards Eeklo, one or two escapes did develop in the beautifully windless, misty farm country, but you had to be a true nonentity like Ad Tak to be allowed very far down the road. Hardly had Tak been reined in at De Cat than we had the gull-like cry of Jan Govaerts and Johnny de Nul's replacement, Van Gestel, disappearing into the stillness. Their lead was soon large enough for us to slip in behind and sample something of their tenuous joy; these Wellington-shod farm people they exchanged winks with; these vast, thunder-and-cloud coloured cows propped against bare tree-trunks. Then at Tiegem, exactly where the similar escape in Het Volk – but going the other way – was caught, Govaerts and Van Gestel were swallowed up. The hours of illusion had ended.

How fitting, too, that the old square mountain of the Kwaremont, familiar from Het Volk and Kuurne-Brussels-Kuurne, should introduce the beginning of hostilities; Raas, deserting his preferred fourth place, led the pack over the top, followed by Ludo Peeters and the recent Flèche Brabançonne winner, Eddy Planckaert, a sign of Raleigh dominance. A descent into open countryside and here we were, an 80 to 100 strong peloton, approaching the swarming humanity of the Koppenberg, several thousand parked cars of it.

Could this 150 m long cobbled ridge be the 'cochonnerie' Bernard Hinault so objects to? But where only Raas and Anderson were to emerge on their bicycles from the 1 in 4 climb in 1984, a twenty-man break now developed. A cyclocross exercise across another 3 km of cobbles and here we were ascending the Taaienberg, the roped lines of shrieking spectators reminding our driver of the anguish that greeted his large Peugeot 504 when it appeared on the heels of a bunch of tiny Fiats during a climb on the Giro. By the top, as Anderson hammered away, the twenty had been whittled down to nine, and the Tour of Flanders had assumed its definitive shape.

There they were in their virtual finish order, Raas, Peeters, Sergeant, Nulens, Haghedooren, Pollentier, Van der Velde, Anderson, the only difference in the next 130 km being that Duclos-Lassalle, victim of a slight crash, would be replaced by Luc Colijn. But a race doesn't manage an overall record-breaking pace of 41.76 kmph unless there is considerable pressure being brought to bear. For well over an hour, across six hills, the advantage wobbled between 30 seconds and a minute, and it wasn't until the execrable cobbled Paddestraat at Velzeke was reached at the 202 km mark that the nine-man lead doubled to a decisive two minutes. One sign of how fast they were going, despite the harrying tactics of the four Raleighs in the chasing platoon, is that it took Luc Colijn 12 km to bridge a 40-second gap (earlier Tommy Prim had come within 100 m). And Colijn on the strength of that became for no less an authority than Eddy Merckx the new white hope of Belgian cycling.

One can criticize Anderson and former winner Pollentier for not leaving it to the Raleighs (Raas, Peeters and Van de Velde) to finish what they had helped start. But, as Anderson said afterwards, just being in the break in an event of such amplitude was the all-important consideration. And that break had to be established. The miracle is that in all those 150 km not one of the nine punctured. It is doubtful whether a commando any smaller would have survived those first two hours.

The ending was a Raleigh formality. We expected Peeters to attack to set up Raas. Instead it was Raas who pulled away 16 km from the Meerbeke finish. That 'JR', as he is known in Belgium, managed to win by a solid minute and a half, despite attacks by Sergeant and Pollentier, shows his intelligence, and the way he and his Raleigh team utterly dominated the race.

GHENT-WEVELGEM

Sandwiched between the Tour of Flanders and Paris-Roubaix, Ghent-Wevelgem is more often viewed as a training race than a true classic. (In 1984 De Gribaldy whisked Kelly off to the Tour of the Basque Country so he could train without the distractions of the Belgian Press.) There have been some, even like the future Paris-Roubaix winner, Dutchman Hennie Kuiper, who have preferred to train alone for seven hours rather than endure the long slog up in the wind to the sea port of Ostend and along the dunes to La Panne where, at the turn inland for the Kemmelberg, the race traditionally begins. But a race of echelons, with a pack split by the wind into successive pursuing waves, is not without its attractions, especially if you have never had the chance to see one in

Ghent-Wevelgem 1983: an echelon forms in the rainy, exposed conditions during the earlier section of the race

Leo Van Vliet
shows the emotion of his only classic win

year, at the same point, the same thing occurs, must leave more than a few team managers grinding their teeth. Nonetheless there were a number of pre-race favourites like De Wolf and 1977 winner Hinault who found themselves inexplicably stranded when the echelons formed in the 1983 race. Others like Sean Yates made it up to the only echelon that counts in such races – the first – only to wind up in a field, and with a broken wheel for his pains, as the *bordure* narrowed with a shift of the wind.

Where in the Tour of Flanders there are thirteen *monts*, in Ghent-Wevelgem there is only one, the Kemmelberg. The Kemmelberg is no bigger than any other Flemish *mont*, but in the flatness of the surrounding plain one does sense its strategic significance, and why it could have changed hands a full three times during the First World War. Reason enough for the race to attack it from every conceivable angle.

At the end, as we hurtled down to Ypres, the even-money choice Raas stood well surrounded by four team-mates in an 18-man lead bunch. A Merckx would have picked the plum; a classic, after all, is a classic. But Raas, as much for the humour of it as to save himself for Paris-Roubaix, decided to launch Leo Van Vliet with 16 km to go.

By now Van Vliet's legs felt as if they were made out of wood. But a master's command is a master's command. And off on his own the big tow-haired Dutchman sped, to reach Wevelgem weeping copiously with the joy of his first big victory. There, too, 20 seconds behind was the winner of the bunch sprint, Raas, telling him as they dismounted, 'Leo, I've never seen a *jump* quite like yours – that slow.'

PARIS-ROUBAIX

Paris-Roubaix is, after Bordeaux-Paris, the oldest of the still extant classics, dating from 1886. The 'Hell of the North' is not to all tastes, and there are a number of riders, among them past winner Bernard Hinault, who see it as little more than an exaggerated form of cyclo-cross. And undoubtedly a race over ancient cobbled roads preserved for this one event as national monuments and which requires bicycles with specially raked forks, saddles lowered and pushed back for stability, heavy touring-weight tyres, and foam inserts under the taped handlebars to lessen the shock to the arms, may strike one as a bit abnormal. But the list of past winners is without exception a roll-call of the great champions of the sport and it's not for nothing that Paris-Roubaix is considered the queen of the classics and carries the most Prestige Pernod points.

Superficially Paris-Roubaix resembles the Tour of Flanders in its 272 kilometres and in the extent of its cobbles. But the Paris-Roubaix cobbles are in the flat rather than on hills (where the water tends to run off them) and they go on almost continuously, it seems, from the moment they are breached at Neuvilly, around the 100 km mark, until 10 km from the Roubaix velodrome. From the spectator's point of view the great thing about cobbles in the flat lies in the way they soak up the rain, gradually acquiring a patina of mud that turns them into a virtual skating rink. Now, on the appointed April Sunday let in a sparkle of sunlight or snow and you may have as glorious a race as you are ever likely to witness: one, it seems, that consists of nothing but catch-catch-catch

Riders in Paris-Roubaix enter the penultimate section of the 'Hell of the North' near Orchies

A rain-submerged pre-modern road poses problems in Paris-Roubaix

On the Wallers-Arenberg forest road, which dates from about 1750

*Two Paris-Roubaix winners: Hennie Kuiper and
Bernard Hinault*

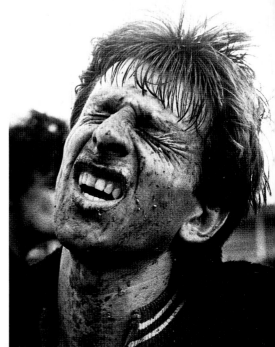

*Paris-Roubaix finisher Paul Sherwen
shows the agony of completing the race*

(or the attempt), emotions exploding one after another off the windshield, motorcycles overturning, riders coming by your own stranded car, falling, coming by again. Because the pack is broken up and the riders are, for at least half the race, out on their own – racing! – it is all totally visible: riders silhouetted against the wind of these great bleak First World War landscapes (much of the race goes through the countryside of the Battle of the Somme); the cobblestones glinting against brick farmhouses, the riders against the massed knots of Sunday-suited or parka-clad spectators grouped in incredible numbers like gulls at a beach. Paris-Roubaix is more than just a race; it is a celebration of a whole way of life, of what it means to live and try to survive in the economically depressed North of France. All this suffering and courage coming together makes for a unique spectacle. But obstacles by themselves do not make a race. A brisk tempo is needed to give a mountain, two or three kilometres of cobblestones, their organism-searing impact. And this Paris-Roubaix has had almost from the moment of its inception outside Louis XIV's great hunting palace in Compiègne.

FLÈCHE WALLONNE

The rivalry between the Flemish and the French-speaking Walloons could not be more intense. If Walloon cycling does not have anything like the density of top riders that one finds in Flanders, they still believe they can put on every bit as good a race. And in the Ardennes hills they possess a countryside much more suitable for racing as it is normally understood. Both the Flèche Wallonne and Liège-Bastogne-Liège are superb races in their own right. They have the added merit of being able to indicate who the on-form climbers are to watch for in the forthcoming national tours.

The younger of the two, the Flèche Wallonne, was originally conceived in 1936 as a way of linking French-speaking Belgium's two furthest cities, Tournai and Liège. Since then the 'arrow' has undergone quite a few changes of trajectory before finding what one hopes to be a permanent home in Huy with its famous 18 per cent 'wall'. This identity crisis was not helped by the classification system that linked it from 1950 to 1964 to Liège-Bastogne-Liège in what came to be known as the 'Ardennais Weekend'. One can see the logic: if the stage racing season begins with these two races, shouldn't one unite the two to create a mini-stage race counting for the Super Prestige? But two races of this magnitude run back-to-back is a lot to demand and the riders inevitably found themselves choosing one or the other. The way out was for the Flèche to become what it is now, a mid-week race.

Since moving to Huy in 1983 the race has been helped no end by the emergence of local hero Claude Criquielion as 1984 World Champion. Criquielion needs a tough, hill-studded course if he is to stand a chance and the organizers duly provided him with one in 1985 as he scored a notable victory. And he might well have won Liège-Bastogne-Liège, but for being stopped on the last hill by some jammed motorcycles. If so, that would have made him the first to complete this rare double since the Swiss Ferdi Kubler did it, for the first time, in 1951-52.

LIÈGE-BASTOGNE-LIÈGE

Whereas the cobbled classics recall the mud and trench warfare of the First World War, this oldest of the Belgian classics – it was first run in 1892, a year after Bordeaux-Paris – takes us directly into the Second World War's 'Battle of the Bulge' (or the Ardennes). The first half of the race around the Ourthe and Salm river valleys and across the plains is apt to be uneventful. At the turn, after Bastogne, the tempo picks up drastically, sparked by the efforts of the various commandos trying either to make a long break, or get ahead where they can help relay should their team leader succeed in breaking away. But Liège is still far away as even Eddy Merckx found in 1971, when his five-minute lead evaporated in the last 30 km (although, absolutely exhausted, he still managed to hang on once caught, and win the resulting sprint).

After the Houffadize climb comes a section of narrow roads growing gradually steeper in wooded hillside before a sharp descent begins at the village of Wanne. The struggle to get to the front here normally splits the race in two because everyone knows that at the bottom, on a sharp right-angled turn, begins the brutal kilometre-long Stockeu wall. From here the road loops back to the cobbled Stavelot village square to begin the longer, if not so steep, climb of the Haute Levée.

By Alpine standards the hills here are not very high, coming up to no more than 550 m. But the swiftness with which the Rosier, Vecquée, Mont-Theux, Redoute, and Des Forges follow one another, at a more and more frenetic pace, means that once dropped hardly anyone ever gets back, even though the last of these, Les Forges, is still 30 km from Liège. How crucial a role these hills play may be gathered from the fact that three-quarters of the victories have featured a lone escapee – a statistic that not even Paris-Roubaix can begin to approach.

Unlike international races in France and Italy which are run by a single organization, these Belgian races are all run by different organizations. The fact that they are vying with one another for popularity can make for very good races (unlike Milan-San Remo and the Tour of Lombardy which are living on their past). But it also means that the promoters have to work against each to garner the sponsors and advertising they need to pay for their races. Since the publicity and international prestige is directly related to the number of journals carrying accounts and photos of the race, it becomes all but impossible to limit the number of cars and motorcycles following the race.

Of these Belgian classics, Liège-Bastogne-Liège – the only one not run by a newspaper, but by a cycling club, the oddly-named Royal Cyclist's Pesant Club Liègois – is perhaps the most strapped for funds. The Club president and race director Emile Masson is the son of a coal-miner who won Bordeaux-Paris in 1923. Masson himself won Paris-Roubaix at the age of twenty-three in 1939, only to be conscripted into the army four days later. Imprisoned by the Germans in 1940, he spent five years of the war in a POW camp, and still had enough left to win Bordeaux-Paris himself in 1946.

For all his prestige, Masson has found it very difficult to raise his race's annual £15,000 budget. Liège, a coal-mining centre, has been in a prolonged slump and the municipality has been able to advance only a tenth of the budget, a sum matched by lgian television for transmission rights. The remainder has come from such sources the national lottery, *Het Laatse Nieuws*, the General Bank, and *Sport 80* (a sports ekly), but with very little margin Masson has not been able to reject enough of the requests for official accreditation. The result has been that there have been more cars and photographers' motorcycles than roads as steep and narrow as these can handle. Again and again breaks have had to come to a complete halt, riders have crashed, and the race itself has been unacceptably falsified.

The photograph facing shows the key event of the 1985 race. As Phil Anderson prepares to attack in a repetition of the move that came so very near to winning the 1984 edition, he finds himself being brought down, whether by a spectator or a stopped motorcycle is hard to say. From the resulting crash three riders, Criquielion, Roche, and Argentin managed somehow or another to slip through. But Criquielion's own later attack was stopped by a further congestion of motorcycles, leaving Argentin, who is far and away the best sprinter, a fairly easy victory.

NATIONAL TOURS

After Liège-Bastogne-Liège there are still some very good classics: the Amstel Gold Race in Holland, Frankfurt's Henninger Turm, the Zurich championship, not to mention the marathon Bordeaux-Paris. But it is now in mid-April the turn of the stage races to come to the fore. These include week-long events such as the Dunkirk Four Days, the Tour de Romandie, and the Dauphiné Libéré, as well as the three-week-long national Tours of Spain and Italy; all part of the build-up that will climax in the mid-summer Tour de France.

These national Tours are decathlon-like events, featuring a complete panoply of the disciplines that make up the sport; time trial, mountain time trial, team time trial, climbs in various ranges, bunch finish sprints, intermediate sprints, etc. Although the national tours are differently slanted – the Vuelta favours the climbers, whereas the Giro d'Italia has evolved a bonus system favourable to the sprinters, and the Tour de France features a lot of time trials – each wants a genuine all-rounder to emerge as a victor rather than a mere specialist. Although the course map varies considerably from year to year, under a general obligation to include the whole of the country within, say, a ten-year period, the same general battle-points tend to recur, if not always in the same succession: the Dolomites and the Apennines in Italy; the Alps and Pyrenees in France. It is these that give the race its character.

The outstanding feature of the Tours is their great length. I don't know whether, as some doctors claim, riding the Tour de France is more strenuous than running a daily marathon, but they are very long and it is very rare indeed that a rider is strong enough to ride all three of them. The length also puts a premium on consistency. Many riders can climb as well as anyone else one or two days in a row; it is another matter to keep it up for a week or even longer, as in some recent Tours de France. This need for

The La Redoute hill is the strategic point in Liège-Bastogne-Liège. Here, in 1985, the congestion caused some leading riders to fall, substantially affecting the overall result.

consistency demands, on the whole, a different sort of physique from that of the classics rider – generally smaller, more slightly built. But these slightly built riders still have to be strong enough to time-trial. It is the combination of these two disciplines, climbing and riding against the clock (both events a spectator can see), that make for a good stage rider.

In the early days of the Tour de France, when the stages were more inclined to marathon lengths than they are today, every other day was a rest day. Now the rest days have been practically eliminated, as in several Vueltas of recent vintage; and in the Tour de France they occur so late in the race as to be practically useless. On the other hand, the Tour de France feels it compensates, as far as the ordinary rider is concerned, with time trials, on the assumption that a rider who is not in the reckoning, or whose personal pride is not at stake, will ride it like a training ride; whereas the others, those with pretensions, need to be and should be stretched to the breaking point.

With the length, the pace, the size of the day-to-day demands, and all the strains of riding in a large pack, there are probably no sporting events that begin to compare with the Vuelta or the Tour de France. Just to survive and finish is extremely difficult. That so many do a good deal more than that, competing to their maximum and at times even beyond, is rather awesome. With them the sport of giants comes into its own.

VUELTA

At a mere nineteen stages the Tour of Spain, the Vuelta, is the first and shortest of the three great national tours. But Spain possesses a considerable variety of mountain terrain and the new organizers have used it well to construct a race that for sheer roughness gives the Tour de France a good run for its money.

It's not so much the course itself that is hard (though nineteen days without a rest is, as Greg LeMond remarked, a bit much), as the Spanish attitude towards racing. The Spaniards tend to be built on the small side. Pounding a gear on the flat and coping with the wind don't particularly interest them. But as soon as a pass comes into view everyone attacks. Whereas in a Tour de France mountain stage you have at most ten or twelve riders at the front, here you will see 40 with attacks raining out, one after another. Most of this is wonderfully chaotic, with the Spanish teams more concerned with making it difficult for another than ganging up against the foreign invaders. And the excitement of the last Vueltas has sparked a marked resurgence for Spanish cycling.

The 1983 Vuelta is typical of those of recent years. Bernard Hinault won it at the price of not being able to race seriously again for the next ten months, a Pyrrhic victory if there ever was one. The organizers had secured the Breton's participation by offering him a reputed £40,000 in start money. Hinault had gotten himself in shape, topping it off by winning the Flèche Wallonne a week before the start. To back him up, manager Cyrille Guimard brought to Spain the strongest possible squad, including Laurent Fignon and last-minute replacement Greg LeMond.

But the Spaniards, Marino Lejarreta, Alberto Fernandez and Julian Gorospe, were

Claude Criquielion, the surprise winner at Barcelona of the 1984 Worlds

A two-man breakaway climbs up to the Sierra Nevada in southern Spain

waiting for Hinault and the first week in the Pyrenees was, by the Breton's own admission, the most difficult of his career. And it was only at the last stage that a gutsy performance – in view of the now almost unmanageable tendonitis – gave Hinault the Vuelta for his hardest ever major Tour victory.

The world championships, Barcelona, 1984: Robert Millar leading Marino Lejarreta

As far as the eye can see... spectators await the Tour of Spain on the outskirts of Madrid at the midway point of the 1986 edition

TROPHÉE DES GRIMPEURS

What more genial way to celebrate Ascension Day than with a *Trophée des Grimpeurs?* This international open climbers' championship, billed as a mini Tour de France, takes place at Chanteloup-les-Vignes, a half hour to the north of Paris and a few twists of the Seine from Monet's Giverny. Like most criteriums it is a relatively short race, just some twelve laps of a six-mile wooded hillside circuit. What gives it its Ascension Day possibilities are the presence of two climbs: one, near Andressy, of 200 m, which rises slowly before turning into a veritable 1 in 5 wall; the second, a kilometre later, averages 1 in 6 for 3 km of under-the-trees, spectator-packed enlightenment before dropping away on a 3½ km descent to the hamlet of Maurecourt. The 2000 m of afternoon climbing that this adds up to may not be the Ventoux in the amphetamine-defying July blaze, but the repetition of effort on a circuit that never gives the riders time to recover – or to relay one another satisfactorily – can make for some notable races, such as that in 1979 in which Zoetemelk surprised Hinault, and the one a year later won by Raymond Martin, a presage to his superb form in the 1980 Tour.

Giro d'Italia

As a nation the French pride themselves on logic. If you want a race, you need a course that offers a few challenges. Everything possible is done to step up the pace and establish a climate of nervous uncertainty in which things have to happen, hour after hour, day after day. The Italians are much less hectic. If a stage finishes in one place, it starts there the next day.

Whereas the French want a continuous battle, the Italians see nothing wrong with a lot of sprint finishes. How boring TV is, they argue, with a motorcycle-mounted camera following the same one or two pairs of fleeing legs. Better a full pack in all its hungry, hydra-headed immensity bearing down on the finishing line: all that mayhem of swerving bikes, jutting elbows, and pushing hands. Why employ so many of the best sprinters in Europe if they are not to be given the opportunity to display themselves? A race in the mountains may be the stuff of legends, but no Italian in his right mind wants to see a 5ft 6ins dwarf or a tall bony cadaver mount the final podium. Racing is beautiful and it is only right that the *begli uomini,* the Mosers, the Visentinis, be given every chance to win. So you slow it down, add a substantial amount of time trial mileage, and top it off with an illusion of mountains. That is a typical Giro of recent years.

Whereas the Tour organizers have always insisted that the race comes first, the more star-conscious Italians have seen nothing wrong in designing the Giro as a showcase for the man of the moment. In 1983, after his victory in the Goodwood world championships, this was Giuseppe Saronni; and a generous system of sprint bonuses was duly introduced – without them Roberto Visentini would have won on overall time. A year later the man of the moment was Francesco Moser who, using a newfangled bike and the newest scientific preparations, had just cracked Merckx's world hour record; so a Giro was duly cut to his measure. On the flattest Giro in recent history Moser duly won, but the manner of it left much to be desired. Even Moser's come-from-behind final stage time trial victory was shadowed by the antics of an RAI helicopter blowing against Fignon and pushing Moser from behind.

The 1985 Giro was expected to yield a three-cornered battle between Moser, Visentini and Fignon's ex-team-mates, Hinault and LeMond. Here, it must be said, reputation counted rather than any specific pre-race results. Moser, a single appearance in Paris-Roubaix excepted, had spent the whole spring season training on his own. Hinault and Visentini had done nothing until finishing second and third respectively in the concluding Tour de Romandie time trial a week before. LeMond, after a better than usual early season – he should have won both Tirreno-Adriatico and the Tour des Pays Basques – had gone home to the Sierra foothills to prepare himself – but there is a gap between 'should have' and actually winning, and some observers felt that the Californian's business preoccupations, his new domestic responsibilites and his million-dollar three-year contract had sapped his resolve.

So there we were in Verona, the city of Romeo and Juliet, for the 6.8 km prologue that began on the medieval Scaliger bridge and finished a few hundred metres away in the shadow of the 25,000 seat Roman arena. In Italy a prologue offers some of the pleasurable distractions of a fashion show. Below our balcony serenely harmonized bikes and jerseys wheeled: small, Columbian-coffee Indians; strident, blue-orange Spaniards; Atalas enclosed virtually down to their knees in revolving blue-and-white barber's pole rings; blue and white vents of the Prim-and-Argentin-led Sammontana Bianchi, the black lettering looking half dissolved in the water of the surrounding blue – and lovely jade-green Bianchi bikes; Saronni's yellow-jacket wasps (the innovation here was solid disc wheels in delicate red-white-and-green national colours); Dromedario with their dark blue handlebars echoing against an otherwise silver frame; most elegant of all the Murella-Rossin, a single red bar setting off a vertical, zebra-striped jersey. Why can't a beautiful sport be suitably attired?

Among all this chic the *pièce de scandale* was provided by Visentini's space-age Piranha. Designed by Arrigoni, it combined roundly plunging ox-horn handlebars with a welded metal motorcycle-like frame: a tall wheel, startling Ferrari-red at the back, plunging onto something white of about half its size, puffed out like a hubcap in the shape of a pouch. How something so patently un-aerodynamic could handle wind had everybody bemused.

In the time trial, urged on by the 60,000 strong crowd and clocking a brilliant 51.483 kmph, Moser finished 7 seconds up on Visentini, 8 on Saronni. Hinault lost 15 seconds, LeMond 21 and the recent Tour de Romandie winning time triallist Tommy Prim 34. Of the first fifteen all had bikes with rear disc wheels, and all except three of these, LeMond among them, had front disc wheels mounted as well. That's how complete a revolution Moser's hour record has made in the sport's technology. Disc wheels seem certain to become to cycling what a spinnaker is to sailboat racing. If the wind is right and the course, like this, virtually curveless, you are going to have to use them, ugly and dangerous as they are.

The first major battle point in the 1985 Giro was the 225 km Pinzolo-Val di Gardena stage. By Tour de France standards the two climbs involved – the 1745 m Costalunga pass followed by a reasonably sharp climb to the ski station finish – were not particularly terrifying. But 225 km is a long way to ride on a first day in the mountains, especially in a pelting downpour that, at moments, could be seen blowing almost horizontally. It was not surprising that no one attacked in the first 160 km. Just surviving, staying on the bike at the pace, took concentration enough.

We were convinced that this was to be the Giro of Giros – when nothing, absolutely nothing, would happen – when, at the bottom of the beautiful Val di Gardena climb, with about thirty riders still together, the pack was suddenly convulsed by a series of attacks from Australian Michael Wilson (working to set up Marino Lejarreta). For a while the pace was so intense that Hinault himself feared he was going to be shelled out. As Lejarreta attacked, more contenders were dropped, among them Moser, Contini, Prim and LeMond. Then, exactly where Fignon had suffered a mechanical mishap in 1984, Lejarreta found himself stalled with a jumped chain. With a considerable effort the Spaniard got back to what was now only a five-man group: Hinault, Baronchelli, Visentini and Swiss Hubert Seiz. The climb, with only three short, hard sections in a not particularly steep gradient, was exactly suited to Hinault. Also to his liking was the

The Giro d'Italia on the way up the Val di Gardena in the Dolomites

petrifying weather, reminiscent of some of the Breton's finer moments, like his ten minute victory in a Liège-Bastogne-Liège raced in a blizzard. As he acknowledged later, 'If the weather had been warm, I doubt I'd have made it.'

For an astonishing 6 km Hinault poured it on, no doubt suspecting this was the one chance the Giro offered of outdistancing Moser. Behind, never more than 3 m back, Visentini gritted his teeth, knowing that the Pink Jersey was his by 45 seconds over Hinault.

After a long schuss out of the Dolomites and down to Vittorio Veneto, the Giro hurtled south, crash by crash, towards the Foggia rest day. In the wet narrow streets of Vittorio Veneto the worst was averted only because a little group had one by one slipped away and there was nothing left to sprint for. Two days later on the outskirts of the Adriatic resort of Cervia some sixty riders fell. Moser with his track experience managed to elude it, while Hinault found himself saved by his new quick-release Look pedals. By the time Visentini had extracted himself – he had some ten bikes on top of him – his margin over Hinault had been reduced to 20 seconds.

So far we had seen a jab, an acceleration or two, but apart from the one climb of Val di Gardena nothing resembling a real race. It was with a distinct pleasure we heard Greg LeMond announcing that for La Vie Claire the Giro was going to begin that day. And it was nice to see his eagerness next to Visentini in the front starting line. But for several breath-taking minutes it looked as if the Giro was never going to leave the Gulf of Taranto city. Torriani apparently had not received his £45,000 fee. Torriani has the manner of a man who is everybody's friend, but when it comes to collecting money he can be a lion.

Just beyond Scandale, the sprint for the first mountain prime provoked a fifty-rider break. By the Crocetta pass, three hours further on, the fifty were down to fifteen, with another small group collected around a far from sparkling Hinault. Moser and Saronni were 50 seconds behind. The descent to the Tyrrhenian port of Paola had the long switchbacks that a time triallist as agile as Moser can use to his advantage. By the finish he had cut the gap to a mere six seconds.

In the key Maddaloni time trial Moser lost to Hinault, with LeMond in third place. Further back at 1:42 was Visentini, the victim of a chest cold. With Hinault securely in the Pink Jersey, Moser was now obliged to contest the finish sprints in an attempt to reduce Hinault's two-minute margin to a minute before the last day's Lucca time trial.

Superficially, the finale we were heading into looked very similar to that of 1984. Then, Moser trailed Fignon by virtually the same minute and a bit he was now trailing Hinault. But then Moser possessed a bike that was a second and a half faster per kilometre than Fignon's; whereas Hinault, with his borrowed carbon fibre wheels, now had the technological edge. Lightning rarely strikes twice in the same place. Moser did get roared home by his beloved *tifosi* to a time trial victory in Lucca. But his 48 kmph effort proved only seven seconds better than Hinault's. Despite a fanatical crowd spitting at him and throwing beer cans and tacks on the road in front of him, Hinault kept his form and his dignity to win his third Giro d'Italia.

Michael Wilson

1986 winner Visentini rides here in second position as the Giro d'Italia goes through the centre of Merano

Francesco Moser and his tifosi

Race director Vicenzo Torriani – 'when it comes to collecting money he can be a lion'

The Giro d'Italia has much to be said for it. Good starts and finishes within the city proper, police efficiency, concern for the welfare of both press and riders, compares with anything the Tour de France has to offer. But day in and day out the Giro is boring in a way that few stage races ever are, or can afford to be. There is a lack of available talent and the course itself is tame. It seems designed so that nothing will keep a Moser or Saronni from winning. Commercial pressures have taken over the sport, so that today Italian teams exist purely as a vehicle for a single personality. This 'star' racer hires a team composed exclusively of domestiques whose job it is to see that he is safely conveyed to that place 20 km or less from the end where he can exercise his finishing talents. When in a twenty-team race you have fourteen committed to not racing for themselves and not allowing anyone else to race, you get the blocked crawls that typify any recent Giro.

And as if this climate of *catenaccio* were not enough in itself to smother a race, the newspapers exert a similar pressure. In Italy the papers have eyes only for the stars, and never for someone from the ranks.

BORDEAUX-PARIS

It is 2 a.m. on a balmy last Saturday in May 1983 in Bordeaux. In the Cours du 30 Juillet only a few insomniacs still loiter about, savouring the starlit sky, the mild wind blowing up from the Gironde two blocks away. Little to suggest that in an hour the oldest, longest, and probably most misunderstood of the great classics will get under way for its second to last time (in its ancient derny-paced form).

How much preparation the 588 km 'Derby' demands is a matter of debate. Towards the end of his career Jacques Anquetil rode and won the Dauphiné and Bordeaux-Paris back-to-back, with only two hours' sleep in an aeroplane in between, a feat that must go down as one of the greatest in cycling history. At the other end of the scale there was two-time winner Francis Pelissier who believed in setting aside three months to prepare the event, '600 km to ride,' as he quipped, 'and six months to recover from it.' Paul Sherwen tells me that the Redoutes for their part have been training for over a month, building up the extra 2,000 km they will need by riding 60 km before a race and another 60 afterwards, occasionally behind a derny motorcycle. 'But you can't ride that often behind the derny,' he adds, 'because it takes such concentration.' The race is notoriously dangerous: André Chalmel's horrible 1982 accident virtually ended the 1979 winner's career; a whole score of riders and derny drivers have been killed or seriously maimed in what was long considered track racing's most crowd-stirring event – because of the noise, and the nature and danger of the chases.

The race falls at a time of year which puts it in conflict both with the Giro and with the mountain work a rider needs if he is to ride a good Dauphiné and Tour de France. Add the expense of an event that requires a back-up car, two derny drivers (including one who has been employed for over a month), a masseur and a mechanic, and the nature of the special aptitudes required, that is, endurance and the ability to ride behind

'Beppe' Saronni – Moser's chief rival

a derny (a track skill, basically), and one can see some of the factors that have reduced the 1983 entry to a mere seventeen in an event that has many of the hallmarks of a prison break thriller: riders who have staked not only their season, but their whole career on success in this year's race.

At a later than usual 3.20 a.m.– French television prefers a prime time 5 p.m. arrival, even if it drastically curtails the night magic – we are off. With the help of a tailwind the pace is brisk – at 37.9 km average for the first seven dernyless hours. Bodies to a man rise out of the saddle on the hills, pool forward in a continuous stream like a team time trial on the left. Why spend any more time in the saddle than you absolutely have to? You feel their camaraderie, the crackle of jokes caught as we emerge from an all-night café. An hour or so later, as *L'Équipe* reporter, Michel Nait-Challal, naps in our front seat, Sanders rides over and with his left fist gives his window a healthy rattle, 'No sleeping on the job!' At this hour people are still few, mostly silent middle-aged twosomes, and truckers standing in front of their pulled-over trailers.

Suddenly comes disaster: Sherwen's front wheel collides with Dutchman Martin Havik's back wheel. Such is the force that Havik requires a new machine, but it is the British rider who is more seriously hurt. Sitting on the road he can be seen pointing to his torn right cuissard shorts, seemingly in no hurry to rejoin the race. His right palm is also badly lacerated. But abandoning a race is not something a rider ever gets to decide about from the ground. The mechanic props Paul back on his bike and with a push off he goes, paced back by Bondue, who has used the time to obey a call of nature, and Van der Haute.

At Poitiers, with a noise like a swarm of bees, the bulbous-bodied derny drivers roar in and a new 360 km long, organism-searing race begins; one in which the usual considerations of mileage, minutes ahead, mean nothing, because everything changes so fast, fast being the 55 kmph average at which everything is now proceeding. It's start and stop. You accelerate, you hit a pace, then you force to your very limits again. This notion of limits is always there, blood bursting in ears. One talks of drugs, and the seemingly inexplicable accelerations and relapses that make this race the true equivalent of Paris-Roubaix may be caused by something one is swallowing, that instant recognition in the stomach each rider knows. But you don't need a drug when you have this yellow deafening bumblebee machine blasting your senses.

This is a race that, more than any other, demands morale. You have to be on good terms with yourself. And, making it more complex, you are not alone. There are all these reflections, team-mates pedalling alongside, the man in the car behind, the horde of spectators on the road, and they all shine back at you. The trick is not to shut them out as one might be tempted to, but to use them, make their energies work, so that when you go, you really mean it.

After 20 kilometres comes the first, three-man attack. Patrick Clerc, working for Tinazzi, leads it off and almost immediately Sherwen, with Huerzeler on his tail, responds. But Sherwen, after briefly drawing level with France's best Six Day rider, finds himself – along with his shadow Huerzeler – giving ground until within a few more

Gilbert Duclos-Lassalle, winner of the 1983 Bordeaux-Paris, riding in Paris-Roubaix

miles he is reabsorbed in the pedalling file. Though Clerc will stay away for another 224 km, Paris is still too far off for the real race, the race for home, to be launched. Everyone else waits, watches, not wanting to put themselves on the line before they absolutely have to. Above all they are watching Duclos-Lassalle, the one item of proven strength among them.

A hundred kilometres have elapsed when Peugeot's Hubert Linard, acting as much on his own behalf as to take the pressure off Duclos, launches the race. A sweet-tempered, elegant rider, Linard does not have the bull-like strength of a Duclos-Lassalle. But he can handle himself behind a derny, a not inconsiderable achievement in a wind that at this stage along the Loire is blowing at gale force. And, having ridden the race already five times, he knows what he is doing (as he was to prove in winning the 1984 edition). Riding exactly to the side of the derny – such is the cross-wind – the Lyonnais rider's advantage grows to three minutes. There for another 20 kilometres it stabilizes as, first, Durant, then Bazzo, are forced to set the pace. Then, with a sudden burst, Linard accelerates past a tiring Clerc into a new lead of his own. If no one reacts, he has won Bordeaux-Paris, provided of course he can hold on to the finish.

At the 440 km mark, exactly where he had abandoned the race a year ago, and just as Bondue is undergoing a change of shoes (always the most painful part of one's equipment), Duclos-Lassalle attacks. The move, with Linard up front, and Bazzo and Tinazzi sucked into the energy-sapping chasing, has the advantage of surprise. Duclos's power is such that in practically the same instant he has a 150 m hole opened up. Behind, the pack, held to that moment by an ever-thinning thread, is in smithereens, and a whole different race, one fully comparable in its sudden reverses, its tidal surges, to Paris-Roubaix, is under way.

Will Duclos-Lassalle last the 134 km to Fontenay-sous-Bois in the Paris suburbs and its three steep, unnecessary circuits? Will Tinazzi reach into his private well and pull out a last burst of something? There is no way of knowing these things and, being Bordeaux-Paris, it is an uncertainty that will last up through the last Saturday-thronged climb at Nogent that leads onto the Fontenay circuit.

But Duclos-Lassalle is not about to let his first classic slip from his grasp. With each mile you see his smile broadening. When his hands go up in a 'V' as he crosses the finishing line the smile is broad enough to haul everybody on the packed hillside into it, glad for Gilbert, and glad for Bordeaux-Paris, that it once more has a champion worthy of it. Sport, after all, is about winning, and when you are as big-hearted as this Frenchman, and have waited this long, the exultation can be of the sort that cracks walls. For this is a race that can reward the hard men for what they put into their vocation, and one that well expresses exactly what endurance is about.

CRITERIUM OF THE DAUPHINÉ LIBÉRÉ

Bike racing, good tabloid creation that it is, thrives on our sense of the sensational. And that's what a stage race does, building up the tension event by event. From the promoting newspaper's point of view the trick, of course, is to invent obstacles, horrors that will interrupt the robot-like churning of a wheel. In the course of a season they come in a variety of forms, from the snow of a Paris-Nice to the mud and cobbles of the Easter classics. But for sheer mind-boggling sublimity it is hard to imagine anything grander than an early June stage race in the French Alps. Unfortunately, the Dauphiné has to compete for media space with the closing week of the Giro d'Italia and with Britain's Milk Race, not to mention the world clay court tennis championships at Roland-Garros in Paris. It is not surprising in the circumstances that people have come to see this climbers' championship as a mere tune-up to the Tour de France, akin to the Midi Libre or Tour of Switzerland, nor that the organizers should make the course adjustments necessary to secure the participation of a Merckx, a Thevenet, a Hinault. But when Michel Laurent, a good all-rounder, but no climber, won the Dauphiné in 1982, something had to give.

For 1983 the new Dauphiné organizer, Marcel Patouillard, put together a course that offered more climbing than the 1983 Giro: a prologue at Sallanches in the shadow of Mont Blanc to set the tone, followed next day by a romp over the Forclaz and a pair of third-category climbs to provide a who's who of those truly involved. Three stages to recover and let the regionals get in their own low sprint blows, then back-to-back, the two big G's of Alpine cycling, the Glandon and the 2600 m Galibier, followed a day later by the most feared of them all, the Ventoux.

In the absence of three-time winner Hinault, the reigning favourite was the recent Amstel Gold winner and Tour de Romandie runner-up, Phil Anderson. Based on past performance, the main opposition appeared to be coming from Greg LeMond, who was being held out of the Tour because of his age and for whom accordingly the Dauphiné offered a primary objective. Anderson displayed his good form by taking the Sallanches prologue on the 1980 world championships circuit, and LeMond confirmed his challenge when, next day, on the last hill he used his 15-tooth cog to overpower local man André Chappuis three-quarters of a kilometre from the summit, then successfully negotiated the tricky descent to the comb-manufacturing town of Oyonnax to win by 18 seconds. It was LeMond who, with the help of his team-mate Eric Salomon, did most of the early forcing on the Glandon. He was still leading in the treeless arctic-like meadows of the upper Glandon when 1½ km from the summit, effortlessly like a squirrel scooting up a branch, the green and blue jersey of Robert Alban flashed into view. In a instant the Beaujolais climber had opened a 150 m lead. From a bend ahead we could see LeMond turning round, looking for somebody to react. On the next jackknife bend the reaction came: Millar, same squirrel-like scoot, only vastly more powerful as he overtook Alban and quickly left him behind.

Millar's move assumed another aspect when Pascal Simon, using an aluminium bike with especially light wheels (three pounds lighter than LeMond's, an immense advantage), jumped away in turn. Simon managed to shake off the terrier-like attentions of little Salomon, the only Renault able to take his wheel, and linked up with Millar on the descent. Here Simon's tallness and his bike's lack of rigidity betrayed him. He fell on a gravelled corner, enough to warrant a change of bicycle. Though Millar and Simon descended brilliantly, their 1½ minute margin at the bottom was not enough to keep them from being caught at the Bourg d'Oisans *ravitaillement*, a few kilometres before the start of the Lauteret climb. To the Peugeots waiting to hand Simon, Millar, and

Anderson their feed, the race was as good as over. 'With his time-trialing ability LeMond has the race won.' LeMond might have agreed, to judge from the way he sprinted away three-quarters of a kilometre from the Briançon finish to reclaim the race leadership by two seconds from Simon.

Next day at the foot of the Ventoux, Anderson tried again, but he was not pedalling at all well when LeMond with a lovely seated ease emerged alongside. One could clearly see the Australian's face change from black panic to a distinct glee as he realized the American was not going to shoot by and leave him stranded. For 3½ km, like a pair of brothers, the two climbed, LeMond pumping away with that consistent, even-tempered stroke that so characterizes him.

A mistake, because now behind Anderson, Simon had emerged, leaving LeMond stuck with the lead. This situation was to change further when Millar joined LeMond and Simon (Anderson having been dropped) at the Chalet Reynard ski station. Greg did not have to lead now, a role which fell to Millar. But with the two of them on each side the American was highly vulnerable. Three kilometres from the summit Simon attacked. Pounding a gear of 42 x 18, something he could never have done a year earlier, the Champenois's lead mounted with each turn of the pedals: a minute, one kilometre from the summit, two, at the very steep summit; by the time he had reached Carpentras, 40 km away, it had grown to three minutes.

Next day, LeMond exacted his revenge in the best possible way by winning the time trial for his third stage victory. He would be subsequently awarded the overall victory when Simon and Anderson tested positive in the same event.

TUNE-UPS TO THE TOUR DE FRANCE

After the Dauphiné comes a series of tune-up races, the Luxembourg Tour, the Midi Libre and Tour de l'Aude in the Cévennes of south-western France, and the Tour of Switzerland, all designed to prepare the riders for the mountains of the Tour de France. By now, after four months in the saddle, the body's fat content has been honed to such an extent that the skin is almost pellucid. To limit water loss hair is crew-cut. And every day after a race you will see the ambitious returning to the hills to put another 100 km into their legs. The Tour de France is where their season has been leading and they want to be ready.

The Midi Libre and the Tour de l'Aude are basically the same week-long race, sponsored by different newspapers. Each has a prologue, and because the stage finishes are never on the top of a hill the times registered in these mini-events can often be determining. Often in the second of these, which somehow counts for the Pernod Prestige, there is an Italian presence, a Moser, a Contini, fresh from the just concluded Giro. Someone new to gawk at, what do twenty days on the road do to a rider? And Italians certainly sit well on a bicycle, we think, wishing that the season had more races in which these two streams could be joined.

As for the rest, it is the south-west and life moves to a different song. Policemen drinking in the bars. The clicks of the games of *boules* in the village squares. Grape-hung trellises you lunch under. Four less weeks of winter. The countryside is very pretty, the hills all in vineyards, but so effectively sprayed that it is only above the streets of a great city that you encounter swallows. Everywhere though, the same palpably Mediterranean sense of how time is to be spent; not in a car following a race, but among people, these solid lines of dark-faced, shawled or beret-hatted quaffers, waiting, a bit of sizzling whiteness in glass, for the first hotly pursued rider to appear.

By contrast the Swiss Tour presents a fascinating meeting ground between the Italian teams coming off the Giro and everyone else gearing up to the Tour de France; then there are the Swiss themselves, who naturally have a great deal at stake – the continued life, say, of a team. Reverberating through it all, at one sprint sign after another down the long beautifully engineered roads (raced, though, only on one side), is the solid ring of Swiss francs. With a prize list of 350,000 Swiss francs the event rates as the highest paid after the Tour de France, a fact that does much to explain its continuing popularity. But the wise desist. There is a considerable difference between breasting a pass on your own in first or second place and taking it as part of a lead group, a few places back. It is a sobering reflection, but no victor of the Tour of Switzerland other than Eddy Merckx has ever gone on to win the Tour de France.

After these last tune-ups, the Sunday before the start of the Tour de France, come the various national championships. And for the Irish, Australians, and Americans, there are the consolations of a few days alone in the mountains, checking out a new climb and getting the body acclimatized to the altitude.

TOUR DE FRANCE

In the world of sports the 4000 km, 24-stage Tour de France is unique. It is a kind of latter-day *Iliad,* if that is conceivable, as well as the most gruelling (and for the competitors the most commercially rewarding) of cycle races. Of 210 starters in 1986, 40 per cent would abandon the race – victims of illness or injury. For a rider, merely finishing in Paris can be a life-time achievement.

Much of the Tour's success stems from its position as the mid-summer climax to the cycle racing season. And France still has the unevenly graded roads and variety of mountainous terrain that lend themselves to epic confrontations: day after day of long, steep, multi-pass stages with all their risk of falls on the descents, of sabotage or other forms of betrayal. The Tour is also the oldest established stage race. Most of the innovations in the sport, and a number of the feats that have created the legend of the 'Giants of the Road', stem from it. After eighty years all this tradition builds up to create a definite ambiance. 'A happening', I remember a matronly Dutch lady telling me as we waited among a vast picnicking mob on the Joux-Plane pass. And the race itself serves a definite vacation need: on a July day in the deep countryside what else are you going to do with your kids? Because the Tour roads are sealed off two hours before the race passes (six hours in the mountains), most will have been there a considerable time. Kids will be scrambling around the wheels of the publicity caravan for team caps and free product samples. Others will be running about the hillside like squirrels, looking for a branch, a jutting flagpole or rock that will offer a better view than the next. Families will have discussed this question of site, of which hairpin bend on which of the day's passes, for months, perhaps ever since the Tour route was first disclosed the previous October. As a crowd they are remarkably cheerful, patient, willing to clap anything that moves: the carloads of journalists racing ahead to lunch, the acrobats and clowns of the publicity caravan, the women racers of the Tour Féminin, the press convoy, the Tour riders and the rally-like driving of the team cars.

For them the Tour is as much a travelling road show as a sports event. Just as the riders are pedalling human billboards, every inch of cap and jersey shrilling forth company colours and names, so everything to do with putting on the race, from crowd barriers to computers, comes free. With an estimated twenty million people lining the roads, and a daily television audience of close to a billion people, it's worth it.

It's the presence of this vast, mainly rural, audience that makes the race commercially feasible, as well as assuring the racers the exposure needed to obtain contracts for the lucrative 100 km criteriums that immediately follow the end of the Tour. To sponsors a Tour stage win carries more publicity value than winning a classic. To the rider a stage win will mean a bigger salary next year and bonuses from sponsors. Unlike most sports spectacles it is the Tour that makes riders famous, and not the other way around.

The Tour funds itself mainly through advertising sponsors. The publicity caravan that precedes the race by an hour ploughs in £4,000,000 alone, roughly 60 per cent of the budget. Another 25 per cent comes from the host cities, who can expect to recoup most of it in the bonanza that comes from lodging and feeding the 3000-man travelling armada. The remainder comes from the teams who pay a hefty £25,000 entry fee that more than covers the cost of their expenses.

The race's success has, in turn, spawned a media event that for sheer numbers of journalists is dwarfed only by the Olympic Games and soccer's World Cup. There is this difference: the Tour is constantly on the move for three weeks. How much of this travelling circus is necessary in the name of efficiency, or desirable for rider safety, is open to question. But 3000 men in flight from their families does generate a certain something. And France is still France with a countryside that changes culturally every few kilometres, a still intact peasantry, and restaurant tables that can compensate for a few hours' harried scribbling.

My first experience of the Tour was in 1978 when I followed the race from the start in Leiden, Holland, to the finish. What drew me to it was the chance of witnessing what I had divined to be a genuine twentieth-century epic. I was not disappointed. This 1978 Tour de France marked Year One of the Hinault Era.

Hinault's was not the liveliest of reigns, mainly because his method of blocking any attack and winning in the time trials tended to eliminate the adventure. Hinault was equally good at trading the minor jerseys within the race, best youth, king-of-the-mountain, and so forth, for extra support. In the 1982 Tour the combines were so effective that everyone knew who would be wearing what from the second day's crossing of the Ballon d'Alsace onwards. To have to watch everyone going through the motions for another twenty stages hardly made for very entertaining fare.

Joop Zoetemelk, winner of the Tour de France in 1980

Hinault and Van Impe, first and second in the 1981 Tour, show the strain as they climb the Col du Coq

While crowd and television-viewing figures remained high, many observers felt that the Tour no longer provoked the same passionate following that it had thirty, or even twenty years ago. For one thing the race itself lacked unity, its skips and jumps seemingly determined more by commercial than sporting considerations. For another, it just wasn't hard enough. The spectre of mounting apathy seems to have got the message across. For 1983 directors Goddet and Lévitan announced a return to first principles: a race starting for the first time in twenty years in Paris and taking place entirely within the country's hexagonal borders; one that in the sum of its demands more than rivalled the 1978 race.

Phil Anderson defends his Yellow Jersey in 1982

1983

In an event that aims at a decathlon-like variety one may not be able to turn every stage into a Paris-Roubaix, or a Milan-San Remo type of classic. But one can have a mini-Paris-Roubaix of cobbled horror in the form of a Valenciennes-Roubaix stage, followed a day later by a 300 km Roubaix-Le Havre marathon. For their part the mountains were to be introduced with a 220 km, five-pass Pau-Luchon stage, ridden for only the second time since 1939. For eight days straight, across the Massif Central and through the Alps, the carnage would continue with time out only for a single rest day at L'Alpe d'Huez. If any course could present a challenge to Hinault this was it. But in the process of winning the Spanish National Tour (the Vuelta) Hinault suffered a recurrence of the tendinitis that had forced his withdrawal from the 1980 Tour de France. In his absence, forecasts were divided between the journalists' favourites, old-timers Joop Zoetemelk and Lucien Van Impe, winners in 1980 and 1976 respectively, and the riders' twin favourites, Sean Kelly and Phil Anderson. Kelly had recovered remarkably from a broken clavicle suffered in the last week of March to win the recently concluded Tour of Switzerland, while the Australian had shown his form by breaking away on a solo jaunt to take the other Tour tune-up, the Tour de l'Aude. But as climbers both Kelly and Anderson are too heavily built to be consistent. In a Tour as hilly as this, one had to respect the chances of Zoetemelk and Van Impe, thirty-seven years old as they were, as well as of Anderson's team-mate, Pascal Simon, the declassified winner of the Dauphiné Libéré a month before.

Through Paris and across Normandy to Le Havre, then south to Nantes, the riders jockeyed for position. But by the time the Tour was approaching the mountains the real news concerned not the contest for leadership between Kelly and Kim Andersen, but the extraordinary heat wave in Europe: one that was to produce temperatures of 107°F in Florence, 102°F in Berlin, and would last all the way to Paris, clamping its seal on the race. With the mercury registering 95°F in the shade it's just possible to imagine what the riders were up against in air so much hotter than the blood, on roads melting away under them in a crackling, tyre-destroying goo.

Heat is bad in the middle-height mountains. It hurts less as you rise into thinner air. It may have been the prospect of such coolness that caused the Anderson-Kelly-Zoetemelk contest that we had foreseen to come apart at the first touch of the mountains. Anderson unluckily got caught up in a crash, and by the time they reached the giant 17 km long Tourmalet pass, it was Colombian Patrocinio Jimenez who, closely tagged by Robert Millar, led the way over the summit.

Behind this pair other similar alliances could be seen; and the blond, bespectacled future Yellow Jersey Laurent Fignon had pulled away from Veldscholten (help he would never have received if the Dutchman had thought him the least threat to his leader Peter Winnen), though that still left him 6 minutes behind Millar at the summit. Finally, 8:30 behind Millar at the summit came an eleven-man posse containing the race favourties: Simon, Anderson, Boyer, Zoetemelk, Van Impe, Alban, Winnen, Madiot, Criquielion, Roche, Breu. A further 7 minutes back was the Yellow Jersey, Kelly; by no means out of the race, just having trouble getting his legs to start functioning.

Patrocinio Jiminez is first across the summit of the Tourmalet, the high point of the 1983 Tour

Cobbles on the Tour de France route in 1983

Driving behind the pack, Peugeot manager Roland Berland saw the race slipping out of his team's grasp. Worried by Bernaudeau's attack on the Tourmalet descent, and the size of Jiminez's lead – but not by Fignon – he ordered Bourreau and Roche to go to the front to do what they could to close the gap. It was at this point between the Tourmalet and the Aspin, with Roche hammering away flat-out, that Simon attacked, again and again. It didn't matter that with each fresh acceleration he was tossing his two leaders, Roche and Anderson, back on Berland's windshield. The Tour was there to be won and at that moment Simon, only two minutes behind Anderson on general time, felt strong enough to carry the Yellow Jersey to Paris.

A few minutes later we came upon Anderson, head tilted to one side, mouth gasping for air, weaving from one packed, screaming side of the road to the other in search of whoever had any water to hurl over his head. What he needed was a coke. When he finally got an uncontaminated can he instantly recovered, passing rider after rider on the long schuss into Luchon.

Millar took the stage, 8 seconds ahead of a quickly descending Delgado, for the second ever British victory in a Tour mountain stage. But there 1:13 behind was the new Yellow Jersey Pascal Simon, with Fignon, Bernaudeau, and Kelly parked respectively at 4:22, 5:34, and 6:13. A sizable lead and, given Simon's prowess as a climber, and his comparative freshness, it was hard to see anyone taking that away from him.

But Tours aren't always won on merit. And Simon was unlucky enough to be right behind Boyer, Bourreau and Garde when they tangled during Boyer's attempt to protect the Portuguese rider Agostinho. In avoiding them, Simon and the motorcycle alongside him went into the ditch, with Simon sustaining a triple hairline shoulder-blade fracture.

Simon's subsequent refusal to quit the race can be understood. But it short-circuited what would have been the decisive stage of the Tour, and it left an acrid taste in most of our mouths. The main victims of the decision to let Simon carry on were the Peugeots. Their only chance was to let Roche and Anderson attack on a middle mountain terrain that suited them. Instead Roche and Anderson now found their hands tied by a fear of doing anything that might cause Simon to lose his precious tunic. Without them the race took on a strange lethargy. The others knew they had Roche and Anderson in a box, and they were determined to keep them there.

It was not until after the Cucheron that Simon put an end to his calvary, leaving Fignon the new Yellow Jersey. One may not like the way Fignon inherited Simon's Yellow Jersey without having instituted a true attack. But judged by his own past what

Eric Vanderaerden overwhelmed at his victory in the final stage of the 1984 Tour de France
following pages, top left: A lighter moment in the Tour de France:
Swiss rider Robert Dill-Bundi empties his water bottle over a female soigneur
bottom left: The men behind the Tour de France: race directors Jacques Goddet
and Félix Levitan
top right: Greg LeMond sprints for the summit of the Col d'Aubisque
in the Pyrenees during the 1985 Tour de France
bottom right: Félix Levitan with Greg LeMond, the first American winner of the
Tour de France

Laurent Fignon, winner of the Tour in 1983 and 1984

Fignon was doing in the mountains involved a real transcendence. Whether he could hold his lead over the next day's six-pass, 247.5 km stage to Morzine was anybody's guess. With nine riders within 6:26, the race could still seem to all of us as open as ever.

One can programme a harrowing multi-mountain Alpine stage, but if the riders don't attack, or stop attacking, nothing will come of it. Fortunately in 1983 we had two riders in Jean-René Bernaudeau and Phil Anderson who don't know what it is to give up. On the narrow, long, fall-punctuated descent of the day's first mountain, the

Laurent Fignon cooling off in unconventional fashion after a Tour de France stage

Glandon, the two attacked, taking with them Van der Poel and Van der Velde. After a chase of 30 km the four were finally caught on the lower slopes of the Madeleine, but not without a certain expense of effort from Fignon's troops. It was at this point that Fignon's team-mate Alain Vigneron chose to attack. Vigneron's venture was immediately seized upon by Arroyo, the Savoyard Michaud, and, you've guessed it, Bernaudeau. They were no sooner reined in on the flat than a series of echelons formed in the cross-wind. Belgian racing at its most typical, but an art that Fignon, Madiot and their like are too young as yet to possess. Behind, the Renaults looked as if they were going to founder *en masse*. For a while Poisson led. Then Madiot, dropped earlier on the Madeleine, did what he could to chase. Finally, with his Jersey on the line, Fignon took over.

On the Colombière descent Michaud took off before his local crowd on what was to be a stage-winning move. The first to the Joux-Plane summit behind him were the Peugeot pair of Roche and Millar, the Dubliner showing that he had made remarkable progress in the art of climbing after a week of rubbing shoulders with Winnen, Breu, Van Impe, *et al.* (At the Avoriaz time trial next day he showed that his performance was no fluke by taking second to Van Impe; a showing that was further underlined by an impressive third place, two seconds behind Tour runner-up Arroyo, on the next to last day's Dijon time trial.) But the winner on the time trial circuit, by a remarkable 35 seconds, was Laurent Fignon. 'Whoosh!' said Roche, slumped utterly drained over his bicycle. One can quibble with Fignon's right to his Yellow Jersey, say that Simon would have won it, or that his team-mate LeMond could have. But a performance like that shows that he did not steal his Yellow Jersey. At the end of twenty-two stages a verdict is a verdict and it seems unquestionable that the best man won.

To me, however, the real winner wasn't Fignon, but the Tour itself which was raced with an *élan* that seem unimaginable for a course of its difficulty. At any point, anything seemingly could happen. And there seemed to be a whole new generation present willing to take life into their hands and attack.

1984

As races go, the 1983 Tour de France could hardly be faulted, day after day of sustained unbelievable anarchy. That a comparative unknown, Laurent Fignon, until then a mere support rider for Hinault and LeMond, should have emerged as victor seemed in the context absolutely fitting. But his triumph, however deserved, was overshadowed by the accident that eliminated Pascal Simon at the moment when he seemed the certain winner; and by the absence from the race of Fignon's more famous team-mates: four-times-winner Hinault sidelined with a knee operation; 1983 World Champion and Best Rider of the Year, Greg LeMond, held out of the grind because of his comparative youth.

Against this background one can see how the 1984 sequel, on a similar, if even more mountainous course, could have the air of a true showdown; not so much a race as a 22-round boxing match between France's two greatest riders: Fignon out to show that

Despite losing time here on the Tourmalet, Laurent Fignon went on to win the 1983 Tour

his 1983 victory was not a fluke, Hinault coming back from months of non-racing in an effort to prove he was still the greatest rider of the current era. Which of them could inflict the most punishment, which absorb it? And how would they handle all the surrounding distraction from LeMond, Kelly, Roche, Anderson, Arroyo, Delgado, and Colombian newcomer Luis Herrera, a winged angel who had taken everything in his country while dominating the 1983 Coors Classic.

Hinault showed his form right away, taking the Saint Denis prologue by three seconds over Fignon. The first part of the race, as the Tour swung up towards the Belgian frontier, was enlivened by a suicidal duel between Peter Post's Panasonic-Raleigh team and the breakaway (equally Dutch) Kwantum-Hallen led by Jan Raas, only six weeks out of the hospital following a serious fall in Milan-San Remo. And meanwhile there was Fignon landing the first telling body blow by taking the Alençon-Le Mans time trial by 18 seconds over Kelly and 49 seconds over Hinault (in an event Hinault had always previously dominated). And by the time we reached Pau on the eve of the Pyrenees a look at the classification table showed Fignon leading Anderson and Hinault by a minute, with another quartet composed of LeMond, Kelly, Visentini and Roche lurking a further minute and a half back; figures that do not indicate very much when it comes to a race in the mountains.

Seeing a mountain stage with a photographer, I soon learned, is a considerably different experience from following the race in a journalist's car. Since you are not allowed to shoot from a window you have to pick a spot. So you drive along looking for it, that quintessence of the race, one that will contain the maximum variety of action, of emotions, within the steepest, most awesome of camera angles. The obvious place to see this particular stage, Graham Watson decided, was the top of the first category Core Pass, some 40 km from the Guzet-Neige hilltop finish. There on a meadow's rock, against a background of surviving snow, greens of every hue, tall Alpine lupins, like an eagle you sat waiting for the emotions to arrive: the rolling shoulders; the glazed eyes; the mouths with the asphyxiated tongues curling out of one side. And they did: of the 'Pictures of the Year', a good majority would come from this one skillet-hot, agonizing stage.

Fignon had wanted to attack Hinault at the 5 km-to-go mark, but his coach, Cyrille Guimard, knowing the Breton's ability to grit his teeth and not only overtake, but pull away, made Fignon wait another 2 km when he would have a better chance of upsetting Hinault's rhythm and staying away. As it was, the agony on Fignon's face at that moment, the jaw suspended–'I'm giving it my all, and then some'–remains for me the outstanding image of the Tour. Fignon gained only 45 seconds on Hinault, but a signal blow had been struck.

The effect of Fignon's attack on top of Hinault's earlier time trial defeat was to turn Hinault from a classy boxer into an increasingly desperate bar-room brawler. As a spectacle the contest could hardly have been improved upon. In the heat of the Domaine du Rouret finish, on an uphill circuit, seven seconds ahead of the bunch, there the two of them were with Anderson, toe to straining toe, slugging it out. Instead of playing it safe Fignon kept turning it on, screw after screw. A day later, after Anderson had fallen, badly bruising his chest cage while trying to gain a few seconds on the

Hinault and Anderson fight to stay in contact on the Joux-Plane in the 1984 Tour

descent into Grenoble, Fignon took it upon himself to lead the bunch in. After the rest day, here he was again, lowering by more than a minute LeMond's 1982 Tour de l'Avenir La Ruchère mountain time trial record.

Clearly nettled, Hinault decided to stake everything on next day's relatively short Grenoble–L'Alpe d'Huez stage. On the second of the three climbs, the wall-like Côte de Laffrey, Hinault attacked, blowing out everyone but Breu, Millar, Arroyo, Delgado, and, of course, Fignon. Fignon, too, has his pride and, near the summit, counter-attacked with Herrera. With the help of a tail wind the two broke away, forcing Hinault and Millar to chase. The junction was finally made in the valley before L'Alpe d'Huez. Rather than wait for the mountain, Hinault, the bit clearly between his teeth, set off on his own – into the wind.

It was sheer madness and Fignon burst out laughing when he saw it. By the time the sharply rising lower slopes of the Alpe d'Huez were reached the Breton was cooked. In an impressive exhibition Herrera soared away to win by almost a minute. But Fignon was second, three minutes ahead of Hinault, and the Tour was as good as won. In the shake-up caused by this one stage all the jerseys except Hoste's Green changed backs,

Life up front: Fignon rides comfortably while team-mate LeMond struggles

with Fignon acquiring the Yellow, Millar the mountain polka dots, and LeMond the White as the best novice. The Tour had taken on its definitive shape.

As we prepared next day for the Tour's highest mountain, the Galibier, on the way to the never-climbed La Plagne finish, it might be asked what was there left for Fignon to accomplish. Win a mountain stage? Well, yes, and at the ski resort there he was, cool, cool, bronze concentration. But the surprise was seeing LeMond pull out of the pack to chase an already fled Grezet, an effort that was to leave him coughing horribly in the high air.

How rending this incessant mountain diet was becoming could be seen in such derelict figures as Herrera, twenty minutes down and unable even to dismount from his bike. Equally rending was the sight of Zoetemelk looking like wax death itself, frozen fear in the eyes and teeth rigidly clamped, being pushed and clearly needing it.

Now that the stuffing had been knocked out of everyone – everyone but Fignon – the trans-Alpine stage was ridden at a lope; just as well or there would have been another thirty-five eliminated. Fignon's superiority was such that he could have easily won again, as he was to prove the next day on the heights of Crans-Montana in the Swiss Valais. But team tactics required that he keep guard while LeMond tried to take second place away from Hinault – a plan that might have worked, but for LeMond's missing a curve on the final descent into Morzine and doing a somersault onto the soft river-bank grass.

The final Ville Morgon–Villefranche time trial, ridden over some of the most expensive earth in France, was everything that a Tour de France next to last day should be. Most of us had spent the night by our thousands in the appropriate cellars preparing for it. Late next morning, there we were with chairs and picnic hampers ranged deep up through the vines, or lying five abreast in the gutter. Café banners, 'Down with dope, up with beaujolais,' reflected the prevailing mood. And the course itself, steep and continuously tilting in the best vineyard manner, with oncoming rider views that called for binoculars, was technically up to the occasion.

The form of a Hinault, a Fignon, is so smooth it is not always possible to tell from the roadside how fast they are going. But when Kelly shot by in a curved bolt past the Chiroubles vineyards there was no mistaking what one was seeing. Unfortunately on the top of the hill the throngs were such that he couldn't pass Pascal Simon without risking a fall. And Fignon, starting last, had the advantage of knowing with 2 km to go that he was only two seconds down. Sprinting, he closed to win by a questionable five-hundredth of a second (it was revealed two months later that the stage had been timed manually). This meant that the Green Jersey would have to be settled on the Champs Elysées. There, next day, Kelly gave it all he had, but out ahead of him with 45 m to go was, you've guessed it, Fignon, giving his room-mate Pascal Jules a proper birthday lead-out. Jules, alas, did not quite make it, nipped on the line by Vanderaerden, but Hoste was there, picking up third place ahead of Hinault and Kelly.

In a Tour full of worthy adversaries Fignon's domination was awesome. To know so exactly how to measure his punches, to be willing to suffer in order to deliver them without once straying into the 'red' zone, is something few of us have ever seen. As five time Tour winner Jacques Anquetil wrote in his *L'Équipe* column:

> *Never in the history of bicycling has a rider made so much progress in so little time. He's able to win on any ground and now he adds panache. He could have played it safe, but he would rather take some risks for glory. There is no superlative strong enough when you talk about him. Fignon is a phenomenon.*

But Fignon was not the only 'phenomenon'. There was the rest of his Renault team who won stage after stage. Oddest of all was seeing Pascal Jules, a man of the flat if there ever was one, almost winning two mountain stages. Why didn't any of them win any other events in the remainder of the year? And what about the Renault riders held out of the Tour who similarly dominated the mid-September Tour de l'Avenir?

One answer came seven months later when Fignon, after riding everyone into the ground during the season-opening Sicilian Week, pulled up lame with what was eventually to be diagnosed as ankle tendinitis. In cycle racing tendinitis is a distinctly modern ailment, caused mainly by the big gears currently in vogue, and which may be aggravated by a spate of bad weather. In Fignon's case, however, one had reason to suspect the forbidden hormone preparations (cortisone, steroids) riders use to build up muscle mass. But bigger muscles put that much more strain on the frail connecting links, the tendons. Stretch them far enough and they will grate on the muscle.

Watching 'superman' Fignon flail away day after glorious day on the Tour one felt that sooner or later something was bound to give way. That the tendinitis should occur at the very beginning of the season was the dead give away. Guimard's Renault laboratory, of course, is not the only one going. There are many young riders outdoing their own most optimistic timetables. But when Hinault remarks, after being informed of Fignon's impending operation, 'You'd think Guimard would have learned from what happened to me,' you can't help but feel he has put his finger on the right button. Coming upon Hinault in 1983 after not having seen him since his Tour ride in 1978 I remember being struck not only by the new hairiness, but by the hugely knotted calf muscles, the knots extending even into the lower thighs; legs more like that of a wrestler than a rider. Two months later, after winning the Vuelta, he was to go under the knife for a left knee tendon operation.

Dope is not the only forbidden subject of cycling. But the ramifications of the issue, how we are to judge what we see, what we would do in their stead, and so on, are far-reaching. Sport, like art, is about risk, learning about your limits and potential, and drugs wonderfully focus the whole issue. In recent years the laboratories have expanded substantially the scope of what they are able to test. But if you are only testing five out of a pack (the leader, the first two of a day, and two chosen at random), you leave a lot of latitude for risk-taking. And to announce, as the organizers did after the Tour, that the dope control tests had all proved negative and to predict the beginning of a new era, must strain credulity.

1986

In 1985 the Tour organizers got it wrong. One understands their point of view – they wanted a competition. With Fignon unbeatable in the high mountains, the only way to provide a challenge was to take them away and instead design a course where the all-rounders, Kelly, Anderson, Roche and above all a restored Hinault, could trade blows with him on more equal terms. When Fignon bowed out with his ankle injury it was too late to pop the mountains back in. So for the 1986 edition the Tour organizers made sure of providing a mountain core worthy of its legend. In many observers' eyes they rather overdid it: two Pyrenean stages back-to-back (instead of the usual one); then, after a few days to recover, three Alpine stages with the last two, the seventeenth containing the Izoard and the new Granon, and the eighteenth with the Galibier, the Croix de Fer, and the Alpe D'Huez, being particularly severe. But the Colombian or Millar victory everyone forecast did not come off. Instead we had something a bit more interesting: Hinault and LeMond, both on the same team, going at each other's throats. And the fashion in which they did it not only burned everyone else off – there were fewer finishers in Paris proportionately than in any race since the war – but made for a duel that will surely be talked of for years to come.

In 1985 on the Champs Elysées podium Hinault had promised to help LeMond win in 1986. 'I will sacrifice for him as he has suffered for me. I don't think he will have any trouble winning the Tour de France.' But a year is a long time and Hinault must have had second thoughts about what he was giving away, and to whom. A national treasure like the Tour is not something a Frenchman can give away, least of all to an American. And in those twelve months his long-since-designated heir apparent had done nothing to show he was worthy of such an honour, failing all his major appointments, including the recent Giro. As the start for the Tour de France approached the pressure on him to reconsider, to think of the morale of his fellow countrymen, mounted. President Mitterand himself is said to have got into the act, telephoning him just before the start. Hinault kept his cool. But you don't go to all the trouble of getting yourself into superb shape to ride for second place.

The first part of the Tour, the eleven stages from Paris to Bordeaux, set the general tone – no loafing – and at an average 44 kmph life in the rather oversize 220-man pack cannot have been much fun. The burden of controlling the proceedings fell to Fignon's Supermarket U, the winners of the team time trial. By the time they reached Bordeaux they were all in shreds, including Fignon, still not recovered from his heel operation. Because of the brisk pace there was only one event of note in this preliminary part – the Nantes time trial. Hinault served notice of the state of his form – he had done nothing so far all season – by winning it by nearly a minute from LeMond who, considering that he had punctured, had certainly not disgraced himself. Then there was Stephen Roche, coming back from a season marred by a bad knee injury sustained a sensational crash in the Paris Six Day, whose third place might have seemed auspicious if one hadn't seen his knees buckle under him as he was helped off his bicycle. Equally praiseworthy was Robert Millar, a mere two minutes back from Hinault, a sign of his new ambition following his winter move to Panasonic.

The first Pyrenean stage through the Basque country to Pau was announced as difficult. But with the last climb, the Marie-Blanque, some 47 km from the Pau finish, no one expected the Tour to be determined here. The pace Hinault and LeMond set over the first 'first category' climb of the day, the steep, paved-for-the-Tour Burdincurutcheta ('Cross of Iron' in Basque), was such that Roche and a cadaverous-looking Fignon were both dropped. Further on, after a junction had been made with a group of seventeen who had left earlier, as the lead group approached the Côte du Monument, came the move that dynamited the race.

Hinault at that point decided to go on the offensive, without telling LeMond. And here he was, using his team-mate Jean-François Bernard's attack to motor off, with only the Spaniard Delgado awake enough to bridge across to his wheel. This left LeMond, to say the least, flabbergasted. What was he to do – run his team-mate down? And it left Millar the impossible task of pursuing the fleeing trio, who were bolstered by a Delgado who had agreed to work in return for the border stage victory. While Millar did his business creditably, the trio's lead was already 2:45 at the Marie-Blanque summit and would keep on mounting, despite a late attack of LeMond's, to 4:37 by the Pau finish. That's a considerable time gap and it was hard to see where LeMond was going to find the terrain to overcome it, especially with a determined Badger glued to his wheel.

It might be thought that the prospect of winning the Tour for a record sixth time would be enough for any one mortal. But Hinault's success at Pau, where he had taken the overall lead, went to his head and in trying to duplicate the previous day's feat he rather over-reached himself. His decision to attack on the descent of the Tourmalet with the Aspin and Peyresourde and, above all, the climb to the ski-station of Super-Bagnères still to come, in itself registered an astonishing presumption, given his previous day's efforts. In the heat and with five Colombians, Millar, and Zimmermann willing to chase, it made no sense whatsoever. To his credit Hinault wasn't caught until the streets of Luchon, a feat that would have won him the stage in any previous Tour. The sight of his boss's suffering seems to have genuinely moved LeMond. 'Do you want help, Bernard?' we hear Greg asking, still the good domestique. 'No, you go on, I'm cooked,' Hinault replied. Given their freedom, Hampsten and LeMond pressed home their advantage, taking back on the Super-Bagnères climb every bit of what they had lost the day before.

The effect of all this on Hinault who, it must be remembered, is his own manager, was to destroy any semblance of rationality he still possessed. He attacked, LeMond responded, and the peloton was destroyed – by five minutes on the Alpe d'Huez stage alone. But this had also meant that he wasn't where he should have been when, the day before on the Granon, third-placed Urs Zimmermann decided that the time had come to go on the offensive. LeMond tucked in behind, and the Swiss, never looking back, never thinking even – there was the Alpe d'Huez stage in the offing – motored along in as impressive a display of pure stamina as many of us have seen. LeMond had, in effect, won himself the Tour, but his (and the media's) doubts about a repeat of Hinault's treachery kept suspense alive until the final time trial.

THE CRITERIUM SEASON

After the Tour de France comes a bizarre 'holiday' in the form of a three-week criterium season. During it the riders dash about madly from one farflung venue to the next, cashing in on the notoriety they have achieved during the Tour. For those lucky enough to be invited these contract-paid appearance races are highly remunerative. During this rather brief period a Tour finisher can expect at a minimum to double his annual salary (all, of course, paid in cash).

These criteriums are closed circuit races averaging 100 km. They usually take place in areas through which the Tour has not been able to pass (Holland, Belgium, Brittany, the mid-Loire). The better known, like those at Callac in Brittany or Chaam in Holland, will draw crowds of 60,000 to 100,000. They are there not to see a race, but the Tour riders. And the race reflects this, with breaks arranged to put the jerseys (Yellow, Green, White, Red) in evidence, and the victory going to a Tour rider.

In the course of these three weeks a rider can expect to log some 15,000 km. And the strains of the driving, often with a pair of races in a single day and little chance to sleep, do definitely take their toll – the major reason why riders who have distinguished themselves in the Tour so often have trouble recovering anything like their form in the remainder of the season. In an underpaid profession such sums are not to be cavilled at.

But there seems something definitely wrong in making a rider earn his Tour money twice. Nor can it be in a team's interest to have riders who are contracted over a season playing this sort of Russian roulette with their lives and end-of-season prospects.

KELLOGG'S INNER CITY CRITERIUM SERIES

In countries where cycling is not part of the reigning culture the problem for promoters has been to come up with a form of racing that will allow the sport to be seen on television and thus popularized. In Britain a successful response to this need has been the Kellogg's-sponsored inner city criterium series. These are hour-long races ridden on a small 2 km circuit carved out of a city's historic centre. Barring the odd hill, obstacles are few; but sharp, narrow corners with their traffic cones and bales of straw can do a lot to focus the attention and string out a pack. Now and again a breakaway group will succeed in lapping the field. But in an hour-long race such breakaways are rare. Because most races end in a bunch finish, they are judged on a points basis, with the points accumulating over the series so that there are several overall issues at stake in each race.

Maybe it's the crowds, maybe the chance to put their sport on the map before a live TV audience, but these criteriums are real races, unlike those on the Continent. And they are tactically complex both because of the shortness of the race and the inherent difficulties of organizing a chase on narrow roads where a break can be soon out of sight. Since it is a circuit race, team strength is important. By getting your team-mate into a break, you are able to control the race and set up the final sprint. But who is actually working for whom and why one break succeeds where so many others have failed is very hard for a spectator to determine. This is because there are a number of over-riding alliances, such as those of the home-based professionals against the continental imports who may have agreed to pool their winnings. Then someone like Phil Anderson comes along to throw his own monkey wrench into the works and one may have a race that is a true ratings winner.

There is much to be said for an event that can put a halt to the inner city traffic and allow a city's architectural heritage to be appreciated. For a newcomer to the sport the combination of speed, bodies and colour, and the way the race builds to a climax, can be exhilarating. But an hour-long race is much too short for a sport where the average race is six or seven times as much. If television can edit out laps for the commercial breaks, why can't they do the same for a race of two or three times that length? In that case the spectators could feel they were seeing a race of a certain complexity develop rather than one that is over almost as soon as it has begun. And it would give them time to develop their own crowd dynamics.

following pages: The Kellogg's races brought professional cycling into the centre of London

COORS CLASSIC

In August, midway between the end of the Tour de France and the world championships, comes America's one and only internationally respected stage race, the Colorado-based Coors Classic. As such it provides an appropriate spot to discuss the distinct form of the sport which is American racing.

Queried in a recent *L'Équipe* about the advent of an American school of riding Jacques Anquetil remarked that, though the United States has produced such excellent riders as Greg LeMond, Swiss Tour winner Andy Hampsten, sprinter Davis Phinney, and Olympic champion Alexi Grewal, it was hard to speak of a definite school because the sport was not yet part of an indigenous culture. I think I know what Anquetil means. When an American kid gets his first bicycle, or even his first ten-speed, he does not immediately put his head down and think he is a Greg LeMond. For him the bicycle is primarily a toy, a form of transportation he will have to put up with until he is old enough to drive a car.

While American interest may never reach continental proportions, bicycle racing is and has been for a number of years America's fastest growing sport, with the number of registered riders doubling virtually every four years. More Americans, for instance, tuned into the Olympic road race than any other event. The success of the film *Breaking Away*, the continually expanding TV coverage by all of the major media channels, the increase in the number and quality of magazines devoted to the sport, the impact of such events as the Olympics, LeMond's victory in the 1986 Tour de France, and the Colorado Springs world championships, all point in the same direction. A definite trend is there and it is being consciously exploited by an industry that needs the growth opportunities America represents.

On the racing level one can't help but remark a growing pyramid over the last fifteen years in the number and quality of those racing internationally. From a single figure, Mike Neel, racing professionally in Italy, to Jonathan Boyer and George Mount at the end of the decade, to the present generation of LeMond, Hampsten, Grewal, Phinney, Kiefel, Thurlow Rogers and Roy Knickman there has been a definite progression in numbers and results obtained. On the distaff side the gains have been even more impressive as American women have, by and large, come to dominate the sport.

Some of this growth has been accidental; Neel, Boyer, Mount and LeMond were all self-taught and went to Europe on their own. But the new generation has benefitted substantially from a systematic coaching method developed by Eddie Borysewicz, an ex-Polish national coach, and from first-rate facilities at the Colorado Springs Olympic training centre. To be sure, there have been some goofs along the way, such as the incredible blood-doping fiasco during the Los Angeles Olympics. But given the smallness of the base from which these riders come – largely Colorado and northern California – American riders have achieved a great deal in a very short time. What they lack are adequate races.

This is what makes Mike Aisner's Coors Classic, as it is now known, so important. It is not only the climax of the American racing season, what every rider builds up to, it is also the only international American stage race that has proved anything more than a flash in the pan.

It is here that Anquetil's remarks about the lack of an indigenous base apply. American promoters take one look at the Tour de France and think they can do the same, but the things that make racing what it is in Europe, the roads, the countryside, the weather, the people, don't necessarily have their American equivalent. For one, the distances have to mean something. In Europe 200 kilometres can be the difference between one language, one way of life, and another. In America it is two hours by car. In the same way a race in the Alps or Pyrenees, or a mountain like the Ventoux, offers a very different spectacle from a chain like the Rockies that rises much more gradually. On the one you have to spin, and a climb of the Puy de Dôme or the Alpe d'Huez looks from the bottom as if you are ascending a cliff face. In the New World the climbs are apt to be more long than they are steep and require power, stamina, a firm stomach, more than powers of squirrel-like acceleration. And the roads themselves are apt to be broad, gently graded affairs rather than the snake-like rising, barely two-car-wide lanes one encounters in European racing. In such conditions the sport of giants has to mean something else.

One thing America does have, however, is dollars. By tennis standards $100,000, the prize money for the Philadelphia professional championships, may not seem a very large sum. But it represents eight times the cash listings for Liège-Bastogne-Liège and among continental riders it has been seen as a welcome step forward. Why shouldn't they be offered prize money commensurate with all the other money being invested in the sport?

Until recently the Coors has not had the greenbacks to toss under the racers' wheels in anything like the Philadelphia manner. Like most promotions it has had to start small and add the stages and difficulties as it could. This is why it was for so long an international amateur race: race director Aisner could not pay the hefty start fees that teams like La Vie Claire or Panasonic must ask in order to compensate their riders for the criteriums they are giving up.

THE WORLD CHAMPIONSHIPS

At the end of August and ushering in, as it were, the autumn season, come the world championships: a week of track, followed by another of road racing culminating in the 270 km Men's Professional Road Race.

Within the cycling season these championships are something of an anomaly. In the first place, they can be anywhere: Brno (Czechoslovakia), San Cristobal (Venezuela), Colorado Springs (USA), Goodwood (England), are some of the venues of the last ten years. Up to this point the season has been admirably exact in its calendrical round. At every moment of the year a race is where it should be. Here for the first and only time one steps out of that cadre and into a truly global time dimension. For the riders concerned this can be rather bewildering – and a challenge, an opportunity. One can see, as they step off the aeroplane, the questions surfacing: from the fundamental 'Why did they pick this place?' to the more practical, 'Can we drink the water? Will they run us over on the roads?' For all they know they could just as well be on the moon.

And the racing suits this sense of being nowhere. All of it, whether track or road, is round and round, an endless circling that makes everyone at the end feel rather dizzy–with a Rainbow Jersey at the end of each event, one that the winner will get to wear for all of the forthcoming season. Wherever he goes he is instantly identifiable, the World Champion, the Rainbow Jersey. And this rainbow has a very definite pot of gold attached to it. No less an authority on these matters than multi-world champion Greg LeMond once calculated that winning the Junior Worlds was worth $200,000 to a rider, the Men's Professional Race $500,000 over the length of his career. It's enough to keep your head upright as you go round and round those seventeen laps.

Where most races are sponsored by a commercial enterprise, usually a newspaper, the world championships owe their existence to the national federations (to which all riders, amateur and professional, in one way or another belong). For these national federations the world championships, necessary as they may be, can't help but be a pretext for a grand convention: promoters trying to get their races on the UCI calendar, or the dates changed, rider's agents, bike manufacturers, accessory makers. In comparison to the mountains of food, the flowing champagne, what is actually going on down below on the track, on the road race circuit, can seem–except to the participants themselves–rather minor.

These national federations, supported mainly by riders' fees and advertising contracts, work well enough on the amateur level, the vast minor leagues of cycling. But the professionals are so much fewer and their interests conflict on many levels. These vary from the basic question of precedence, 'Who is living off whom?', to issues of safety such as obligatory helmets. In the world championships the conflict surfaces as an issue of allegiances.

In the Men's Professional Road Race, for instance, the riders represent their countries of origin in the form of twelve-man national squads. But their primary loyalty may well be less to their country than to the trade team which is paying their salary, and which will advertise their victory. The major federations try to get over this by offering the riders victory bonuses substantial enough to knit them together. A sum such as $10,000 a man in the case of the Italians, the Dutch, or the French may make for a disciplined squad; one capable of injecting a sapping pace into the battle and controlling attempts at a breakaway. But money is often not enough to provoke solidarity, and there are squads like the Belgian where everyone will be riding their own race. Carried to an extreme one can have the comic situation of Goodwood in which LeMond chased down Boyer as he attempted to flee with less than 1½ km to go. America clearly was not big enough for the two of them.

The situation becomes even more ambiguous for a rider representing one of the

Eric Vanderaerden in the final stages of the Paris-Roubaix classic

following pages: Sean Kelly leads the Nissan International Classic through the Gap of Dunloe

minor cycling nations, Denmark, say, or Great Britain. The loyalty he has to a trade team and its leader certainly exists; but it may be undercut by the opportunity – and it's the great point of the world championships – to ride for himself. In these conditions a lone wolf can profit from the ongoing rivalries to show his class, as Tom Simpson did at Lasarte in Spain in 1965, or as Freddy Maertens did at Prague in 1981.

Like the national championships that precede the Tour de France, the Worlds is a circuit race. It has not always been such and there are suggestions that the spirit of road-racing would be better served if the first half of the event in which nothing ever happens were to take place on a road going somewhere. That way an element of adventure might be preserved in that it would be much harder to pinpoint, on uncertain terrain, the extent of a breakaway group's lead.

Still, a circuit measuring 15 km gives the riders a chance in a way that the usual 2 km criterium circuit does not. And one can understand why an organization playing host to 900 riders from some fifty-seven countries might need a circuit to which admission can be charged, as against the free space of a road race.

The distance, 270 km, is by mid-season post-criterium standards rather long; all the more so if it contains a climb. A 300 m rise may not seem all that much; multiply it by 18 and one has a considerable mountain.

Most countries have stage races specifically designed to allow their riders to get in shape for an event of this length: the American Coors, the Tours of Belgium, Holland and Britain, the Tour du Limousin and Paris-Bourges. Even so, the Italians inevitably come in as favourites, because their post-Giro criterium season ends six weeks earlier than everyone else's. It is no accident that they have won the Worlds eleven times since it was first run in 1927.

The trick of defending for a team like the Italians, anxious to hold the race together for one of its sprinters, is to make sure that you get one (preferably two) of your team into every break. Otherwise you will be condemned to chase. It is customary for each team, as part of the sapping operations, to designate certain riders to attack early and act as rabbits. The higher the early pace the fewer will be those left around to contest the later laps; a strategy that worked well for Bernard Hinault on the notoriously hilly Sallanches circuit in 1980.

1983 LeMond

Among current riders no one has made more of a career of the Worlds than Greg LeMond (reminding one of how much pre-disposition there is in a name). Junior Champion in 1979 at Buenos Aires, silver medallist at Goodwood in 1982, he became on the beautiful course over Lake Constance a year later the first American to take the Rainbow Jersey. The way he did it on a solo breakaway, taking time from the peloton at

Dutchman Jan Raas wins the Bordeaux stage of the 1984 Tour de France

Champion of France Laurent Fignon holding off Sean Kelly during Liège-Bastogne-Liège

Fallen champion: Freddy Maertens of Belgium, twice world champion, but now a mere shadow of his former self

The Italian squadra *working to bring back Anderson*

each stage of the circuit, was the first indication we had of the true potential of this
future Tour de France winner.

After the muddy humidity of Zurich's Oerlikon, the site of the track events, Lake
Constance seemed like paradise: from the top of the Wartensee, at 585 m, views of
Germany and the Austrian Arlberg; steep orchard terrain with pasture greens that
looked as if they had been lifted out of a watercolour tube; for the hundred thousand
spectators, a 14.994 km circuit that seemed purposefully drawn to take in every possible
beer garden. 'Hard, but fair,' ran most pronouncements on a course consisting of two
sections of climb for a total of almost four kilometres, or 226 vertical metres per lap. In
the threatening atmospheric conditions, however, it was the sharp, slalom-like plunge
from Grueben onto the streets of Rorschach that had the riders worried. 'There'll be
twenty finishers and twenty in the hospital,' Stephen Roche predicted.

As usual the race started out slowly with no attack of any consequence until the
beginning of the ninth lap. At that point Lucien Van Impe decided to take things in hand,
in the process shelling out a fifth of the pack. On the next lap Spaniard Vicente Belda
attacked and the Italians made their great mistake: they got only one man, balding
Mario Beccia, a good climber but no sprinter, into the subsequent seven-man
breakaway, which included some dangerous long-distance riders: Regis Clere, Serge

The winning move: Ruperez relaying LeMond with eight miles to go

Demierre, Kim Andersen, Phil Anderson, and the Dutchman in form Theo de Rooy. With Anderson orchestrating the relaying of Clere, Andersen and Demierre magisterially, and no one in the pack reacting, the break's lead reached 3:23 at the beginning of the thirteenth lap. At that point, rather belatedly, the *squadra* decided to take the chase in hand. But Anderson wasn't to be reined in until the sixteenth lap. As the pack climbed the Wartensee, Alberto Fernandez attacked. No sooner had the Italians roped him in than LeMond attacked, Hinault style, using his 15 gear. He took with him Faustino Ruperez and, as guard dog, the future 1986 World Champion Moreno Argentin, a redoubtable sprinter. On the descent the trio caught and soon dropped Demierre who had struck out on his own a lap earlier. But under Italian pressure their lead soon shrivelled on the next lap descent and it seemed, watching LeMond turn around, only a matter of moments before they would be caught by a pack that had them squarely in its sights. Fortunately for LeMond, Ruperez decided at that moment to turn on the power. By the beginning of the next to last lap they had Argentin gasping for breath. From there on it was a strict two-way contest with Ruperez to his great credit matching Greg relay for relay.

Ruperez has one weakness, an inability to respond to a jump, and on the climb before Wartensee LeMond socked it to him. By then Roche, tailed by Van der Poel, had reacted – as did Fignon a short while later. Though Roche caught Ruperez he couldn't make any headway on LeMond whose lead grew throughout the final climb, the descent and the run along the lake to a winning 1:11 leaving Van der Poel in second place and Roche taking third.

1984 CRIQUIELION

The 1984 world championships on a demanding course overlooking Barcelona was notable not so much as a race – it was too hot – but for the way victory in it transformed the career of twenty-seven-year-old Belgian Claude Criquielion. There have been plenty of nonentities who have won the Worlds and never done anything else. A countryman from the same small-farm background as Kelly – the two were long-time team-mates and remain good friends – and long the perennial hope of a singularly starved Walloon cycling, Criquielion was determined to honour the Rainbow Jersey. He trained harder and he started to win: the Flèche Wallonne in 1985, the Tour de Romandie and the Midi Libre in 1986, and the Tour of Flanders in 1987. In 1986, besides finishing fifth in the Tour de France, he did well enough to be classed as third best rider of the season. Like Kelly, it only took one big victory to transform his confidence and his career.

1985 ZOETEMELK

If Criquielion's 1984 victory was surprising, even more so was Zoetemelk's in the 1985 Montello edition. For my own part, after seeing the Dutchman come apart in the 1984 Tour de France, I could not believe he had anything like another victory left in him, much less one of this magnitude. But Zoetemelk wanted to make 1985, which he then

Claude Criquielion, the surprise winner at Barcelona of the 1984 Worlds

The platoon climbs the Wartensee in the 1983 Worlds; notice the national jerseys

saw reluctantly as his farewell year, a good one and he trained harder than ever during the winter. The results justified this when he won Tirreno-Adriatico (after LeMond had to drop out). And he retained enough of his form to be there on the last lap of this world championships after nine-tenths of those starting had already gone to the wall.

The race was at this point being waged between the Italians led by home-town boy Moreno Argentin and a three-man Dutch brigade, with LeMond cast in the role of the joker. In the flat, coming off the last turn, as everyone hesitated preparing the sprint less than a mile away, we saw this lone figure far over on the left accelerate away; surprising in itself, because Zoetemelk does not possess a true jump. All he was trying to do, he said, was force the Italians to chase and set up a counter-attack for Van der Velde or Van der Poel. But the Italians looked to LeMond and when the American, wisely, refused to expose himself, Zoetemelk was a hundred metres down the road and, with his time-trialling ability, uncatchable.

Almost as satisfying as the victory of this professional's professional of nearly forty summers was LeMond's cool second place in the resulting sprint.

AUTUMN CLASSICS

With the one-day glamour of the World's the season abruptly climaxes. Up to this point everything has had a focus; you rode this race to prepare that one. After the Worlds there is little specifically to prepare, unless it be the time-triallist's championship, the 90 km Grand Prix des Nations, an event that concerns only an élite few. Races are run, of course, stage races like the Tour de l'Avenir, the Étoile des Espoirs, the Tour of Catalonia, the Irish Nissan, classics such as Paris-Brussels, Creteil-Chaville, and the season-ending Tour of Lombardy; but the fires that animate them are, on the whole, personal. A professional has a job to do and he does it as best he can. But most are drained by the effects of a long season, the injuries and cars and roads and hotels and all that goes with it. It is hard to blame them for wanting to go home so that they can start building themselves up for the next season.

The stage races reflect this looking ahead. The mountainous Avenir may be the biggest amateur stage race, and the crucial apprenticeship for the Tour de France (at one time it preceded the Tour by a few hours on the same roads), but as its name implies its slant is towards the future. In the same way the Étoile des Espoirs was originally conceived as a proving ground for professionals too young to have yet ridden the Tour.

If the bulk of the pack, like the public, have their thoughts fixed elsewhere – on transfer news, new teams coming into being – the apathy can always leave room for others to pull off a last coup, or to get some winning habits implanted. Among these may be riders who have been injured and are looking to the autumn classics to salvage an otherwise lost season. Then there is that estimated quarter of a pack who are out of a job and who are more than willing to grab at whatever straws the season offers. This is not the best of all mixtures, but with the help of the Super Prestige Pernod competition, now coming on line, it can be enough to create some notable races.

Autumn sunshine warms the backs of the riders in the 1982 Tour of Lombardy

The Super Prestige is a points competition based on twenty-six major events to determine the year's best rider. There is some quarrelling over what races should be included – those cloudy, yellow-tinted Pernod spectacles naturally tend to favour the French. But there is no doubt that the heavy weighting given to the autumn programme succeeds in keeping the suspense going from the Nations and Paris-Brussels on through to the Grand Prix d'Automne and the beautiful, season-ending Tour of Lombardy. While creating a race outside the race itself, stage-race fashion, it encourages riders to enter international events they might otherwise duck. And the 50,000 franc cash prize (about £4,500) is worth contending for.

Daniel Gisiger of Switzerland, one of the few people to beat Hinault in the Grand Prix des Nations

GRAND PRIX DES NATIONS

After the Worlds the Grand Prix des Nations gives the time trialists their chance to square accounts. Up to now in the season, time trials have always appeared in the context of a stage race. However useful a 'test of truth' may be in such a context, it can also leave something in doubt, since it is the larger race that is providing the decisive motivation.

For the first thirty-five years of its life the Nations was raced on a hilly 140 km circuit to the south and west of Paris, finishing on the now demolished Parc des Princes velodrome. Between 1953 and 1966 it became the virtually exclusive property of Jacques Anquetil, who won it nine times (including once as a nineteen-year-old amateur). Equally remarkable is the manner in which Anquetil, after doing the second fastest time ever in 1953, continued to improve on his record, at whatever the distance, up to his retirement in 1966. In 1956 the distance was shortened to 100 km, then shortened once again in 1964. With the loss of the Parc des Princes velodrome in 1967 the race moved to a number of locations in the Paris area before finding in 1977 its present home in Cannes on the Riviera – with a course that seemed tailor-made for Bernard Hinault who won it five times.

There are other time trial circuits, from those of the Tour de France to the 64 km Eddy Merckx Grand Prix in Brussels (raced a week earlier) and the two-man Baracchi Trophy (for long the last event on the racing calendar). But the double 44.5 km circuit of the Nations is far and away the toughest because of its length and general hilliness. From the start at La Croisette, between the topless beaches and the swank hotels, the circuit rises 300 m within 13 km to the village of Vallauris, before embarking on a further 16.6 km section of short, hairpin climbs mixed with brisk, winding descents. Add the sizzling heat or torrential thunderstorms so often encountered at this time of year and you get a race that provides a very exacting test of just who one is as a cyclist.

PARIS-BRUSSELS

This race of the two capitals is the second oldest of the Belgian classics. It began life in 1893 as a 407 km endurance contest, and even at the present distance of 305 km, it still remains the second longest classic after Bordeaux-Paris. Once very popular, its prestige has never recovered from the seven years interruption between 1966 and 1973 which was caused mainly by the problems of obtaining permission for Sunday racing.

Long races rarely please the riders; especially mid-week ones in mid-September. David Walsh, in Senlis for the 1984 start, caught the mood perfectly; 'Wednesday September 19 was the kind of day when summer slipped into winter, kids realized they were back at school, and the girl at the office noticed that her mid-summer tan was fading.' Walsh also quotes Paul Sherwen, one rider who can put a positive face to almost anything, as saying: 'This is the race that brings on the end-of-season blues.'

It is hard to know whom the first 200 km to the Belgian border are meant to satisfy. There are virtually no spectators on the road and the race itself is conducted at a crawl.

But once across the border and into the Walloon hill country people start appearing in front of their brick houses and the tempo begins to pick up, animated by the Belgian riders and the prospect of a lakeside arrival in the national capital.

NISSAN INTERNATIONAL CLASSIC

The autumn calendar is not rich in stage races, what there are – the Tour de l'Avenir and the Étoile des Espoirs – being reserved mainly for amateurs and young professionals. To fill the gap and give the senior professionals a way of preparing for the last two confrontations of the season, the Grand Prix d'Automne and the Tour of Lombardy, the promoters of the Kellogg's Inner City Criterium Series came up with a five-day stage race, the Nissan International Classic, in Sean Kelly's Irish homeland.

Despite its newness in the pro calendar, the race has been an outstanding success on both a sporting and artistic level, testimony to what one can do in a country where cycling is not a major sport if one has a star of Kelly's magnitude to galvanize the crowds. The knots of spectators along the roads are every bit as dense as at the Tour de France and the racing itself has been fast and highly competitive.

Its success derives not so much from 1985, when Kelly used the classic's first edition as a springboard for the remarkable recovery of form that saw him come from virtually nowhere to regain the Super Prestige Pernod Trophy, but more from the second running of the event. In 1986 the Irishman was pitted against the considerable fire-power of Vanderaerden and Anderson's Panasonics, Zoetemelk and Van der Poel's Kwantums, plus LeMond's La Vie Claire, and had a much harder time. With no time trial to display his prowess in that discipline – Kelly won the previous year by virtue of his world record-beating 32 mph test – he was forced to battle tooth and nail all the way against Canada's Steve Bauer. On the last day, the only one in which he managed to don the leader's jersey, and after barely surviving a downhill crash, it came down to the final sprint of the day in Dublin's O'Connell Street for Kelly to secure victory.

All this genuine drama helped stifle the theory that this new classic was merely a Kelly benefit race. Perhaps only a country like Ireland could have yielded such a probing test. Its geological formation of peat bogs, exposed moors and stunning, now and then very demanding, mountains is one that lends itself to cycle racing. It may well be that the race's strategic battlepoints – the unsurfaced road crossing of the Gap of Dunloe, the repeated climbing of the 1 in 4 St Patrick's Hill in Cork – will one day rank in the same legend as its older brothers, the Alpe d'Huez, the Puy de Dôme, and the Col du Galibier in France. The Irish Classic is certainly proof that, given the right ingredients, a beautiful country can get the sporting event it deserves.

GRAND PRIX D'AUTOMNE (CRETEIL-CHAVILLE)

Creteil-Chaville, or the Grand Prix d'Automne as it is sometimes known – the start changes virtually every year – is the modern successor to Paris-Tours, the old sprinters' championship, and a race almost as old as Paris-Brussels. On the roads of another century a 250 km race to a city like Tours might have represented a considerable test. On

Sean Kelly plays an integral role in the Nissan International Classic; here he wears the leader's jersey in the 1985 edition

modern highways and without a single obstacle other than the wind, there was no way to keep the peloton from arriving all together at the city gates. For the public at large Paris-Tours is simply the one classic Eddy Merckx failed to win (other than Bordeaux-Paris which he never entered). When the race finally collapsed in 1974 no one batted an eye.

Efforts to turn Paris-Tours around and run it back to Paris by way of the hills of the Chevreuse valley did not prove any more successful. In recent years, however, with a new destination in Chaville and an uphill-ending finish (preceded by a sequence of narrow corners that defy a pack pursuit) we have seen some highly complex tactical battles. Moreno Argentin was astonished to find himself cut off in the second peloton and unable to get back when the 1984 race caught fire at the 110 km mark; something, he said, that would never have happened in Italy, and one more proof that the problem of the autumn season lies as much with the courses themselves as the riders' apathy. Give them a course with some obstacles and they will attack, as the Tour of Lombardy has proved time and again.

A mid-race crash during the Nissan International Classic involved a TV motor bike as well as competitors

The unsurfaced road through the Gap of Dunloe makes for a tough climb

TOUR OF LOMBARDY

To many aficionados this season-ending race 'of the falling leaves' is not only the most beautiful, but the best, of the single-day classics. The setting itself, all around Lake Como, is certainly worth an autumnal pilgrimage. The lake may not be quite what it was in Stendhal and Manzoni's day, but with its steeply terraced fields, its rings of mountains and breath-taking views from one or another pink-cobbled promontory, it is hard to imagine a more noble setting for a bike race.

On the eve of the race it is customary to pay a visit to the little chapel of the Madonna del Ghisallo, perched some 600 m above the lake at Bellagio. Until recently this climb was the crucial obstacle of the race, and it was here that the *campionissimo*

following pages:

In one of the most closely fought finishes to a classic, Kelly triumphs in the Tour of Lombardy, but LeMond takes second place to win the Super Prestige Pernod competition

Fausto Coppi fashioned the breaks that allowed him to triumph for four years in a row between 1946 and 1949, even though the Milan finish was some 60 km away.

It is worth noting how often, on a descent, riders are surprised to discover that their childhood beliefs in God are very much intact. In 1948, in response to a request from the Giro riders, Pope Pius XII lit a candle in the Ghisallo church's choir and made the Madonna the riders' patron saint. Today in the flame-lit chapel one can see the atheist Coppi's 1948 Tour de France-winning Bianchi bike hanging next to one of an anonymous *bersagliere* (the Madonna protects all cyclists!), while a wall of honour contains a distinguished palette of coloured jerseys, pinks, yellows, tricolours, Olympic rings, donated by Coppi, Bartali, Saronni and Moser, among others. Another row of marble slabs honours those killed in one or another race, while outside a sculpture commissioned by the Italian Olympic Committee shows a pair of riders, one pedalling along, his left hand raised in a victorious salute, the other morosely picking himself up from his overturned bicycle. It is a singularly moving place.

The paving of the Ghisallo climb in 1958 ended that particular springboard. For the next two years there were bunch sprints, with eighty-five men regrouping in 1959 before the finish on Milan's Vigorelli track. One way to stop the regrouping was to bring the finish closer to the mountains and in 1961 it was moved to Como. This forced in turn a change of route, with the Sormano and the easier side of the Ghisallo appearing at the end of the first 70 km to shed the pack, after which the race circled the lake, with the three determining climbs of the Intelvi and the Schignano (back-to-back) and the much smaller San Fermo della Battaglia appearing in the last 65 km.

This changed route led to some very good races, not least Tom Simpson's victory in 1965 and Merckx's two victories in 1971-72. By then, though, in response to touristic demand, the engineers were beginning to get to work: uprooting the beautiful curve-pattern paved cobbles; blasting tunnels through the lakeside mountains to replace the old, bumpy, at times unpaved, lake-straddling highway. The result has meant that the Intelvi-Schignano climbs, far from resolving anything, have become just part of the last winnowing process. One may not like the prospect of a great climber's race – and with it the super Prestige Pernod competition – being decided by a twelve-to-twenty-man bunch sprint, gripping as that might be. But that has been happening increasingly of late, a tendency sure to be accelerated by the decision in 1985 to move the finish back to Milan, sixty flat kilometres away from the last battle point.

Kelly, Lejarreta, LeMond and Criquielion working together during the climb up the Intelvi in the Tour of Lombardy in 1983

BOOKS ON CYCLE RACING

There are some very good books on the sport in English. Among the outstanding is David Walsh's recent *Kelly* (Harrap), certain to become a classic of sports portraiture, Geoffrey Nicholson's *The Great Bike Race* (on the 1976 Tour de France), and the legendary Australian Russell Mockridge's *My Life on Wheels* (killed by a bus at the height of his career, the journalistically trained Mockridge was one of the few riders who successfully combined a road and track career).

But such good writing hardly begins to approach the wealth of what is available in French. As a language French manages to express what life on the road actually feels like to a rider. One has only to say 'ravitaillement' to be invaded by a sense of all that good nourishment flowing down one's throat, something not at all rendered by our 'feed'. 'Démarrage' (often used accompanied by 'sec', as in wine-tasting) has a brutal forward thrust that 'jump' and even 'attack' don't begin to convey. Nor is the beauty of an 'échappé', of having got away from the accompanying swarm and being out there all on one's own, exactly rendered by 'breakaway'. 'Bidon' to a rider is something a good deal more than a mere water bottle. 'Chaleur', to take a more common word, has a feeling not only of warmth, but of being wrapped in summer like a scarf – a condition where you can bask without having to worry about being chilled to the marrow. On the other side of the ledger there are, of course, some English words for which there is no French equivalent, such as 'sprint', a term expressive enough to have become the title of a French racing magazine.

The historian of the sport is the novelist, Pierre Chany. It was his highly literate 2000-word daily race summary – he is the heir to three generations of a style – that originally made me want to see the Tour de France. He has now followed his two race histories, of the stage events and the single day classics (including the world championships) with an equally monumental history of the Tour de France (Éditions ODIL). The point of view is not exactly unbiased – Chany writes for the sponsoring *L'Équipe* – but he has no equal in his knowledge of the sport and his style is up to the demands of a living comic epic.

More of a writer than Chany, if impossible to translate because of his pun-larded prose, is Antoine Blondin, a winner of France's Grand Prix Littéraire for his novelistic output. From 1951 until very recently Blondin has been following the Tour as a columnist for *L'Équipe* (mostly in Chany's car). These columns are like jazz pieces, written in long-hand after the day's race, and under the tension of an immediate deadline. For those wanting to experience the headiness of that daily breakfast champagne there is his personal anthology, *Le Tour de France en quatre et vingt jours* (Denoel/La Table Ronde). Better still, as an introduction to a planet and a way of life, is his earlier *Sur le Tour de France* (Éditions Mazarine), also available as a chapter in the best of the picture books, *Les Joies de la Bicyclette*.

Roger Bastide is another born raconteur and his *Anquetil, Darrigade, Geminiani, Stablinski: caids du vélo* brings alive an earlier generation than we have known. His early, now hard to find, *Doping* remains – with Andre Noret, *Le Dopage* – the best of what is available on a fascinating subject (Bastide always regarded it as his best book) while *À la Pointe des Pelotons* is invaluable in the way it takes one behind the racing into the commercial structure of the sport, showing the way secondary sponsoring developed from Raphael Geminiani's original tie-in with the vermouth, Saint Raphael, on down to the Bic involvement with Merckx's great challenger, Luis Ocana.

Bastide is also the collaborator in the greatest of the cycling autobiographies, André Leducq's *Une Fleur au guidon* (Presses de la Cité). A great rider of the 1920s and 1930s, and a successful journalist, Leducq is less concerned with recounting his exploits, which he does hilariously, than in getting across in each sentence a point of view and a joy in life. That *A Flower on the Handlebar* comes plentifully spiced with Parisian slang may seem a drawback to some, but if the spoken language is to be learned there can be no better way.

The best book by far on a single stage race is Dino Buzzati's recently reissued account of the Coppi-Bartali duel in the 1949 Giro d'Italia. Buzzati was not a sports fan and, until assigned by the *Corriere della Sera,* had never seen a cycle race (his hobby was mountaineering). And the main event in this Giro, the duel between the leftist, ex-prisoner of war Coppi and the piously Catholic, cigarette-smoking Bartali, takes a long while to get under way, as these things often do in Italy. But Buzzati never lets his attention waver and uses his novelistic gifts to give us a picture of an unique historical moment (six months before the most crucial general election in Western Europe since the war) and an absolutely distinctive psychological combat that shows better than anything I know exactly what this sport at its most intense is about.

Lastly, I must mention the Van Den Bremt/Jacobs-edited Belgian annual, *Vélo.* In a poorly documented sport a book that presents the facts is certainly appreciated.

THE RACING CALENDAR

FEBRUARY

Bessèges Week (France)
Ruta del Sol (Spain)
Antibes Grand Prix (France)
Mediterranean Tour (France)
Valencia Week (Spain)
Laigueglia Trophy (Italy)
Monaco Grand Prix (France)
Sicilian Week (Italy)
Tour du Haut-Var (France)
Sassari-Cagliari (Sardinia)

MARCH

Milan-Turin (Italy)
Het Volk (Belgium)
Limburg Tour (Belgium)
Kuurne-Brussels-Kuurne (Belgium)
Paris-Nice (France)
Tirreno-Adriatico (Italy)
Milan-San Remo (Italy)
Catalan Week (Spain)
Tour of Campania (Italy)
Across Belgium (Belgium)
Harelbeke Grand Prix (Belgium)
Tour of Reggio Calabria (Italy)
International Road Criterium
  (France)
Flèche Brabançonne (Belgium)
Three Days of La Panne (Belgium)

APRIL

Tour of Flanders (Belgium)
Tour of the Basque Country (Spain)
Ghent-Wevelgem (Belgium)
Grand Prix Cerami (Belgium)
Paris-Roubaix (France)
Flèche Wallonne (Belgium)
Liège-Bastogne-Liège (Belgium)
Tour of Spain (Spain)
Amstel Gold Race (Holland)
Paris-Camembert (France)
Tour of North-west Switzerland
  (Switzerland)

MAY

Rund um den Henninger Turm-
  Frankfurt (Germany)
Trophée des Grimpeurs (France)
Zurich Championship (Switzerland)
Dunkirk Four Days (France)
Tour de Romandie (Switzerland)
Tour of Tuscany (Italy)
Tour of the Midi-Pyrénées (France)
Tour of the Mining Valleys (Spain)
Giro d'Italia (Italy)
Tour de l'Oise (France)
Tour of Aragon (Spain)
Bordeaux-Paris (France)
Criterium du Dauphiné Libéré
  (France)
Grand Prix de Wallonie

JUNE

Tour of Luxemburg (Luxemburg)
Midi Libre Grand Prix (France)
Tour of Switzerland (Switzerland)
Tour of the Appenines (Italy)
Tour de l'Aude (France)
National Championships
Tour de France (France)

JULY

Tour of Friouli (Italy)
Camaiore Grand Prix (Italy)
San Sebastian Classic (Spain)
Matteotti Trophy (Italy)
Grand Prix de l'Escaut (Belgium)

AUGUST

Sabatini Cup (Italy)
Coors Classic (United States)
Agostoni Cup (Italy)
Tour of Belgium (Belgium)
Tour of Britain (United Kingdom)
Tour of Holland (Holland)
Tour de Limousin (France)
Paris-Bourges (France)

SEPTEMBER

World Championships
Tour of Catalonia (Spain)
Tour of Venetia (Italy)
Tour of Lazio (Italy)
Eddy Merckx Grand Prix (Belgium)
Paris-Brussels (Belgium)
Grand Prix des Nations (France)
Étoile des Espoirs (France)
Baracchi Trophy (Italy)

OCTOBER

Tour of Emilia (Italy)
Grand Prix d'Automne (France)
Tour of Piedmont (Italy)
Tour of Lombardy (Italy)

STAGE RACES

A stage race like the Tour de France is not one race, but a series of races; for each stage is complete in itself with its own prize money both for the individuals and the teams they represent. The time trials aside, these are conventional mass-start races at distances ranging usually between 160 and 250 km. Each rider's daily times are compiled together to create a general classification (or G.C.). The overall winner or *Yellow Jersey* is the rider who covers the total distance in the least time.

In addition to this overall competition there are a series of races within the race, each with its appropriate jersey: a points competition for sprinters (*Green Jersey*) based on finish positions; the sprinters have also a 'hot points' jersey for the first three across the line at dozens of points along the way; there is a climber's prize (*White-and-Red Polka Dot Jersey*) based on summit line sprints with points awarded according to the climb's difficulty; and a *White Jersey* for the best newcomer. These competitions ensure that there is always something at stake for almost everyone, besides the glory of finishing on the Champs Elysées.

To help enliven the race, there may often be a system of time bonuses, which are then subtracted from the race time. These small parcels of seconds may be awarded to the first three finishers, or the first three at a hot points sprint.

Time bonuses have their drawbacks in that it is difficult for the public to understand what amounts to a whole supplementary system. But in a closely contested Tour a few seconds picked up in this way may be enough to create a new Yellow Jersey, particularly in the early stages before the mountains create larger time differences.